HOW TO ROAST A PIG

TOM REA

From OVEN-ROASTED TENDERLOIN *to* SLOW-ROASTED PULLED PORK SHOULDER *to the* SPIT-ROASTED WHOLE HOG ★ ★ ★ ★ ★

Quarry Books
100 Cummings Center, Suite 406L
Beverly, MA 01915

quarrybooks.com • craftside.typepad.com

First published in the United States of America in 2013 by
Quarry Books, a member of
Quayside Publishing Group
100 Cummings Center
Suite 406-L
Beverly, Massachusetts 01915-6101
Telephone: (978) 282-9590
Fax: (978) 283-2742
www.quarrybooks.com

10 9 8 7 6 5 4 3 2 1

ISBN: 978-1-59253-787-7

Digital edition published in 2013
eISBN: 978-1-61058-770-9

Library of Congress Cataloging-in-Publication Data
Rea, Tom, 1985-
  How to roast a pig : from oven-roasted tenderloin to slow-roasted pork shoulder to the spit-roasted whole hog / Tom Rea.
    pages cm
  Includes index.
  ISBN 978-1-59253-787-7
  1. Cooking (Pork) 2. Roasting (Cooking) I. Title.
  TX749.5.P67R395 2013
  641.6'64--dc23
                                                    2012039054

Design: John Foster at badpeoplegoodthings.com
All photography by Natasha Bidgood with the exception of iStockphoto.com, 13, 14, 15;
Shutterstock.com, 10.

Printed in China

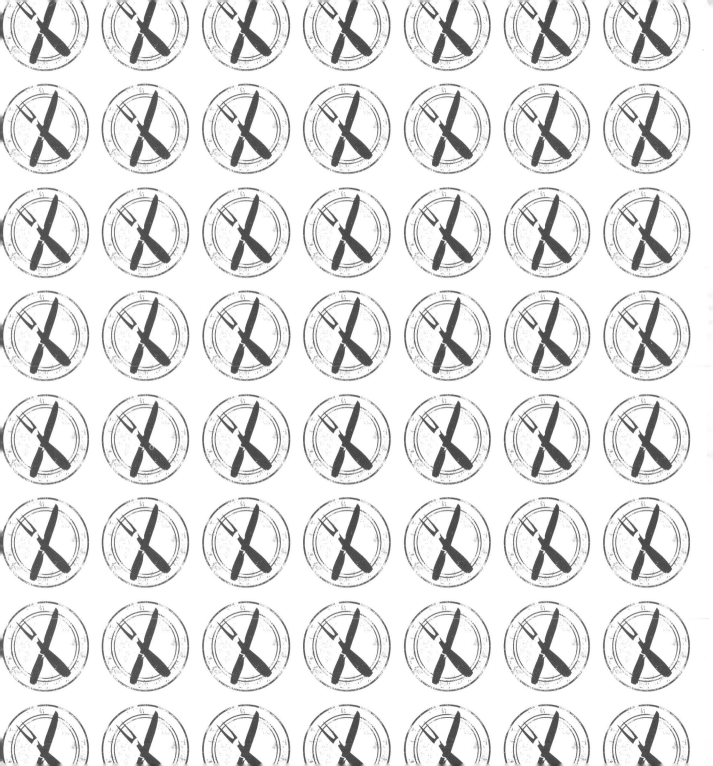

CONTENTS

𝔍ntroduction ★★★★★

Imagine the rich, evocative smell of roast pig hinting at the succulent pleasures to come; the crunch of perfectly cooked crackling; and, of course, the magical *je ne sais quoi* of bacon that tempts even the most stalwart vegetarian. Yes, there's no doubt that pork is the king of meats. Whether slow-roasted belly, pan-roasted pork chop, or the porky paradise of a whole hog, your nose knows when pork is roasting.

This book will teach you the basic roasting techniques in a chef's arsenal—and honestly, they are simple to learn. However, unlike your average cookbook, *How to Roast a Pig* won't simply focus on individual recipes, but instead will help you understand different cooking techniques.

Each roasting technique will give you myriad recipes at your disposal with a small application of your imagination, allowing you to answer the ubiquitous dinner party question, "Which cookbook is this from?" with a true sense of pride as you say, "Actually, I created it myself."

Each section starts with the basics, offering an in-depth, step-by-step recipe to produce a perfectly cooked piece of meat. All roasting techniques are accompanied by two everyday examples of how you can alter the cooking process to change the dish, plus one signature dish to wow your guests. You'll see how easy it is to extrapolate from your newly gleaned knowledge to create unique and tasty recipes of your own—even if you are using up leftovers.

Finally, we'll move on to the joy of the hog roast, covering both spit roasting and the mystical Caja China box. Whether you want to enjoy roast pork as an everyday meal or give it pride of place at a special occasion, *How to Roast a Pig* will make you king or queen of the pork dinner, and the envy of all—especially the guy or gal next door.

CHAPTER 1

Introducing the Pig ★★★★★

I guess that if you have gotten this far, you're not just browsing in a bookstore and you've actually bought the book—amazing! You're almost ready to start making everyone who lives downwind from you very hungry indeed. But, hold your horses; we're not ready to cook quite yet. I know it's tempting to leaf on to the recipes and jump straight in, but, as an older, wiser chef used to say to me, "Fail to prepare, prepare to fail." First of all, you need to understand the pig.

The pig is one of the oldest forms of livestock, domesticated in 7000 BCE from indigenous wild pigs in the area that is modern-day China. The first pigs were brought to the United States by the Spanish in the mid-1500s.

Before the start of selective pig-breeding programs and en masse farming in the twentieth century, pigs were born in the spring, fattened during the summer, and slaughtered at the end of autumn. Due to the seasonal nature of the availability of pork coinciding with apples (harvested in late summer and autumn), a Western culinary tradition was born that still stands today. The year-round availability of meat and fruits has not diminished the popularity of this combination, showing that, "If it ain't broke, don't fix it."

The modern farmed pig is, to all intents and purposes, a man-made creation. This change occurred after World War II. Pig farmers at the end of World War II selectively bred pigs to meet the mass demand for flesh rather than the fat, creating the modern intensely farmed pig that we know today. They used the same natural selection process as Augustinian monk, Gregor Mendel, who between 1856 and 1863 selectively bred peas to show desired traits, becoming the father of the science of genetics.

PIG FACTS

- Twenty-three percent of the world's population doesn't eat pork for religious reasons, and that's before you add in those who don't eat meat and those who can't afford the luxury. Yet the world's population eats 110 million tons (100 million metric tons) of pork a year—the same weight as 274 Empire State Buildings' worth of pork.

- The United States slaughters approximately 1,200 pigs an hour.

- The largest pig ever recorded, in 1933, was called "Big Bill." Owned by Burford Butler of Jackson, Tennessee, he weighed 2,552 pounds (1157.5 kg) and was 5 feet (1.5 m) in length and 9 feet (2.7 m) high. Amazingly, he weighed three times as much as the aptly named Hogzilla.

- Pigs are more intelligent than dogs and rank fourth on the list of intelligence behind chimpanzees, dolphins, and elephants.

- Pigs feature extensively in art (which shows how much we love them). The earliest known picture of a pig is believed to have been painted 40,000 years ago in a cave in Altamira in Spain.

- Pigasus the Immortal was the only pig (it's debatable) to be put forward as a candidate for the presidency of the United States.

Selecting Good Pork

Now this is a difficult section for me. The farmer's son in me wants to tell everyone to eat fantastic, naturally reared heirloom pork—and honestly, it makes a difference. But the practical part of me knows that, especially when times are tough or you want to eat less fat, it's not always possible. Here are four quick tips to help you assess the quality of pork you are buying.

The Skin/Rind

The thickness of the rind can give you a good estimate of the pig's age: the thicker the rind, the older the pig. This is important to check, because not only will it be harder to get good crackling with a thicker rind, but also if the pig is too old the meat will be tougher. The upside of an older pig is more flavor, and the problem of the tougher meat can be negated by choosing a slow-cooking method.

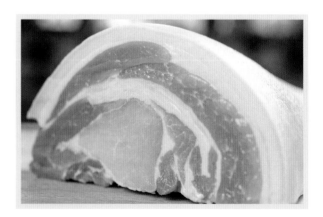

Color of the Meat

You can tell the freshness of pork by the color of the flesh. Checking this is more important with pork than with other types of meat because the degradation of the flesh is much faster. What you are looking for is a nice light pink. However, heirloom pig flesh will be darker than that of a standard farmed pig.

Check for paleness coupled with little blood speckling in the flesh, because blood speckling means the pig was stressed before it was killed. Excess stress during the slaughtering process will cause the meat to be tougher, be less flavorful, and, in extreme cases, have a pronounced acidity in flavor.

Smell

This is an obvious one: if it smells bad, it is bad in most cases, so don't eat it. Cryo-packed meat is the exception because inert gases are used to ensure there is no oxygen for pathogens to grow. This is only the case if it's been vacuum packaged by a major manufacturer. To get rid of the sulfuric smell (if it's in date and not obviously spoiled), take your meat from the package, rinse it under cold water, and leave it to air-dry for 10 to 20 minutes. By this point, the smell should have all but gone if the pork is good to eat.

Fat

This is what makes pork taste and smell so good, as well as stay moist. You are looking for a good covering of pure white. Discoloration of the fat is a sure sign that the pork is of poor quality.

The Provenance of Pork

Worldwide, pork is one of the most popular meats on the table, but some consumers' avoidance of pork due to concerns about dietary fat has prompted producers to breed leaner pigs. These pigs are also bred so that they grow much faster than usual, allowing quicker turnaround and greater profits but providing slightly different results.

Farmed Pigs

Farmed pigs are fed a restricted diet and produce lean, cheap meat that is fantastic for making pork a healthy everyday meal (trimmed pork loin steak, pound for pound, has the same fat content as skinless chicken breast). Because of this leaner pig, the resulting pork is lacking intramuscular fat, and some of the qualities appreciated in pork are lost. Lean pork has less flavor, and the lack of marbling through the flesh can make it dry and stringy after cooking. But you still can't knock farmed pork for what it is: cheap, lean, with a good deal of flavor—it's a product of consumer demand.

I'd rather eat it than intensively farmed chicken, because pork still has some flavor to it. Put it this way, you don't hear anyone describing some bland form of protein as, "Tastes like pork."

In short, the modern farmed pig is readily available and the choice for you if you're:
- On a budget
- Looking to eat leaner and healthier
- Looking for a specific size and weight for a spit roast
- Can't get heirloom pigs easily

Heirloom pig

Heirloom Pigs

Heirloom breeds such as Berkshire, Duroc, and Mangalitsa have become more popular in recent years as people search to eat pork that isn't "the other white meat." Due to the pigs' varied diet, their meat is rich tasting, juicy, and tender, with flesh that is dark, earthy, and full of flavor. Some cuts contain as much fat as they do meat

(bad for your waistline, fantastic for your taste buds). The pigs are smaller, take longer to reach slaughter weight, and bear fewer piglets in each litter, thus greatly increasing the cost to the farmer to produce, hence the higher price. Heirloom pigs have started to cause waves in the food world because their meat is unctuous, succulent, and decadent. Eat as much as you can before heirloom pork becomes a trademark like Copper River salmon and Wagyu beef, and the prices skyrocket.

Heirloom is the pig for you when you're:
- Looking for more flavor
- Opting for moister meat
- Able to afford it
- Not worried about its effect on your waistline
- Concerned about whether the pig had a truly natural life

Wild Boar

Wild boar is not farmed, so quality can vary massively between pigs. Due to this, it is wise to steer clear of boar until you understand the basics of meat quality control. However, boar is a fantastic treat for anyone, albeit a little harder to cook than pork.

The texture is similar to pork, but there is little fat and the meat has a fantastic gamey taste because of the animal's varied and natural diet. As such, you can treat young tender boar like pork, basting liberally to ensure the meat stays moist.

Wild boar

While looking for a piece of meat, you may have the option to have it attached to its surrounding bones ("on the bone") or have them removed ("off the bone").

Meat that is cooked on the bone will:
- Be more flavorful
- Suffer less from shrinkage as it cooks
- Be harder to carve

Bone-in cuts are ideal for smaller gatherings, because the bone makes it look bigger and more impressive, and it is worth gaining the extra flavor. However, the bone is going to slow down carving and serving the meat, especially during large meals.

Meat that is cooked off the bone will:
- Be less likely to be a problem for fussy guests
- Cook more evenly
- Be simple to carve

Any meat from an older animal requires a bit more care because, if treated incorrectly, it can be dry to the point of being unpalatable. To avoid this, pot roast or slow roast your meat and baste, baste, baste to ensure there is plenty of fat to keep your pork moist. Marinating is a fantastic way of tenderizing meat in general, but it is even more important with boar.

The primary reason, from a chef's point of view, to roast pork without the bone is that it makes it so much easier to cook a large joint evenly while also making it much easier and faster to carve. As such, boneless joints are the prime choice for a large dinner party or gathering.

Jointing a Pig

Although this section is called "Jointing a Pig," butchering a whole pig is a book in its own right. Instead, I'm going to take you through the pig, breaking it down to six sections: shoulder, loin, belly, leg, ribs, and other bits. Knowing which part of the pig a cut is from gives a good indication of its qualities, meaning that you can select the correct cooking method to obtain great results.

HOW MUCH DO I NEED?

Now you know what kind of pork you want to buy. The next thing you should ask yourself is, "How many mouths do I have to feed?" This differs from cut to cut, so use this portioning chart to calculate how much you'll need. Once you have decided which cut to use and how many people you want to cook for, calculating the amount to buy is simple.

Number of people ÷ portions per pound
= weight of meat needed
e.g., 20 people eating country-style ribs
20 ÷ 2 = 10 pounds (4.5 kg) (minimum)

A word to the wise: It is always good to order a little extra because there is nothing better than leftover meat for sandwiches, and nothing worse than running short.

Cut	Portions per Pound (2.2 kg)	
Blade/Boston butt, bone-in	2	
Blade/Boston butt, boneless	3	
Picnic/shoulder joint, bone-in	2.5	
Picnic/shoulder joint, boneless	3	
Blade loin, bone-in	2	
Top loin, boneless	3.5	
Fresh ham roast, bone-in	3	
Fresh ham roast, boneless	4	

Cut	Portions per Pound (2.2 kg)	
Ham, bone-in	3.5	
Ham, boneless	4.5	
Pork belly	3	
Back ribs	1.5	
Country-style ribs	2	
Button ribs	1.5	
Spare ribs	1.5	
Shank	1.5	
Sirloin chops	3	
Rib end chops	3	
Boneless chops	4	
Tender loins	4	
Picnic steak	3	
Blade steak	3	

Boston butt

Picnic ham

The Shoulder

Shoulder of pork lends itself to the slow and low techniques that are the most forgiving of all roasting methods. This makes shoulder cuts fantastic for a variety of occasions, especially if you aren't sure exactly when people are going to be ready to eat, because you can easily lengthen the cooking process by a couple of hours without detrimental effects.

The shoulder can be broken down into two separate halves, the top half being the Boston butt and the bottom being the picnic ham. This area of the pig does a lot of work when the pig is alive, being in continual use. This means that flesh is a little tougher, and has more connective tissue in the muscle fibers. However, the shoulder has a great fat covering around the flesh and fantastic intramuscular marbling. If cooked "slow and low," it will give you tender, moist meat, with a lot of the fat either melting into the meat or being rendered off, thus avoiding large amounts of fat under the sumptuous crackling.

However, pretty much all the joints from the shoulder still get good results when cooked with a more intense heat method if you use a few simple tricks, which will be covered later. When looking for a joint or cut to high-heat roast, you should look mostly to the joints from higher up the shoulder, such as the Boston butt and blade steaks, because there are fewer bones, ligaments, and tendons to cause an unpleasant mouthful.

Loin cut, middle

Loin cut, back

Loin cut, front

The Loin

This is probably the most readily identifiable cut, with back bacon (bacon taken from the back as opposed to the more common belly area), chops, and roast loin being among the most widely consumed pork products in the United States. It is characterized by the large round muscle (the eye of the loin) and a good solid fat covering over the top, called the back fat. The muscles of the loin run along the top of the ribs and around the spine, meaning that most of the cuts can be cooked on or off the bone.

Because the muscles in the loin cuts are among the least used during the pig's life, this is where the most tender cuts of pork come from. They lack the intramuscular fat of all the other areas of the pig, so the soft texture of the meat makes loin cuts a great choice for the fussy eater.

Despite the lower fat content, these cuts of meat remain juicy if cooked properly and to the correct core temperature, but they will dry out quickly if subjected to prolonged heat (unless cooked in a liquid medium). These cuts really need to be cooked for as short a time as possible, so you'll get the best results if you oven roast, pan roast, or cook on a medium-high barbecue.

This is also a good part of the animal to use if you are on a restricted diet, because loin cuts have a great meat-to-fat ratio if you remove the back fat. Center-cut steak and pork tenderloin cuts are especially lean, making them a flavorful replacement for chicken breasts in a low-fat diet. If you're not looking to be super-healthy and you

Belly slab

keep the back fat attached while cooking, not only will it help keep the meat moist, but it also makes fantastic crackling.

The Belly

Comprising belly and spareribs, this is possibly the best eating part of the pig, if treated correctly, and it is also one of the cheapest.

Pork belly is the most amazing piece of meat in a pig because it's comprised of nonworking muscle (very tender meat) with plenty of well-distributed fat (loads of flavor and moisture). The reason that it is cheap is that it has too much fat for most people. To make meat from the belly into amazingly mouthwatering pork requires a much longer cooking time to allow the excess fat to render from the meat, requiring more time to prepare than most other cuts. Honestly, it's worth it.

A whole ham

If roasting a large joint, slow and low cooking will allow the excess fat to melt from the flesh, leaving you with a succulent, porky delight. This method works equally well on smaller cuts (e.g. family roast for four); but steak-style cuts from the belly, such as belly strips, can be cooked by one of the quicker methods, especially pan roasting and barbecuing. Because the flesh is innately tender, and as long as the belly has a less than 50 percent fat-to-meat ratio (which should only be a problem with heritage pork), it's amazing barbecued. Cutting belly into slices/steaks across the layers of fat increases the surface area, which helps the fat escape quicker.

The Leg
The leg of pork is partway between the well-marbled and fat-covered shoulder and the tender, lean loin cuts of meat, but that's not a bad thing. It makes the leg of pork the most versatile cut of the pig, because it produces good results from

Rack of spare ribs

both slow and low and higher heat methods of cooking. Obviously, it will never be as soft and juicy as well-cooked loin or as meltingly moist as shoulder, but it's still really good eating.

The leg of pork is also known as the ham, because this is the joint of the pig that is most commonly turned into its namesake by curing and sometimes smoking. Generally, the basic curing process uses salt and sometimes sugar to draw the water from the flesh of the pork, which intensifies the natural pork flavor while also tenderizing the meat.

Most producers of hams add other ingredients such as bay leaf and juniper to their cure to create layers of complexity in the overall flavor and really make the meat sing. The leg has a wide range of cuts available, such as gammon (ham) steaks (great for pan roasting),

Shank

ham hocks (pot roasting), and whole and half hams (roasting). Cooking a ham follows the same principles as cooking pork but with a slightly shorter cooking time due to the reduced water content.

Ribs

Although all forms of ribs come from previously mentioned areas of the pig, they don't fit with the cooking characteristics of the meat from those cuts.

Spareribs are the most common ribs that you will see. They consist of eleven to thirteen long bones (depending on the size of the pig) taken from the belly of the pig to just behind the shoulder. There is a good covering of meat on top of the rack as well as between them, and they are the least expensive cut of ribs. You may have heard of St. Louis–style ribs and Kansas City–style ribs. These are merely variations on spareribs, with the name referring to the way in which they are trimmed.

Cheeks

Trotters

Baby back ribs are sometimes referred to as loin ribs, because they are cut from the loin of the pig. They have a covering of meat over the bones, and also between them. They are shorter, smaller, leaner, and considerably more expensive than spareribs.

Country-style ribs are actually not ribs at all, but loin chops from the shoulder end of the loin, right behind the upper portion of the shoulder. They are more like fatty pork chops than ribs. Although they have more fat per pound than any of the other styles of ribs, the fat is in layers and the meat between those layers is leaner and less marbled than in most other ribs. They are the meatiest of all the ribs.

Everybody knows that ribs are best on the barbecue. However, they are also amazing roasted in the oven.

Other Bits

The other parts of the pig that are less commonly used but just as interesting include the shanks and hocks, cheeks, and trotters.

SHANKS AND HOCKS

Pork hocks and shanks are the lower part of the legs of the pig: the shank is the front leg of the pig and the hock is the rear.

The shank offers a generous portion for one, while a hock should give you two reasonable portions. Both contain two round bones exposed at both ends and are best cooked slow and low, gently releasing the flavor from the fat and the bone into the meat, while allowing time for the tenderization of the meat to occur.

The hock is a great piece of meat packed with flavor and really cheap. On top of this, because the picnic and the leg are used in ham, the hock is available as both fresh cured and smoked, making it a really great way of eating for less while still maintaining variety.

Cheeks

These tasty morsels from the pig's head need long, slow cooking in liquid to tenderize and soften the meat. They're incredibly flavorful and meltingly tender when braised or stewed.

To release the full potential of these wonderful pieces of meat, they are best pot roasted, because the fat and gelatin will enrich the dish and make a smooth, velvety-textured sauce with a sticky finish. They are relatively hard to get a hold of, but if you can they are a great way of eating pork on the cheap (my butcher quite often gives them to me for free if I'm buying meat). They are also amazing for dicing into stews.

Trotters

Some people love trotters. I am not one of them. I'm not squeamish; it's purely that there is very little meat on the average trotter and what you do find is relatively gelatinous compared to the rest of the pig and not worth fighting for.

On the other hand, pig's trotters are amazing when used alongside bones in stock and sauce making. Just roast them in a pan and put a couple in your stockpot if you're making stock, or use them as trivets (placed underneath roasting meat to ensure that the meat is not sitting on the bottom of the pan) so that when you make the gravy for your meat, some of the fat and gelatin are emulsified into the sauce, adding to the flavor and creating that slightly sticky, palate-coating sauce that you get at great restaurants.

If you do want to cook with trotters, get a different book, because I've never tasted a recipe that was worth writing about.

Basic Equipment

We'll soon be into the kitchen porn section of the book where evocative words and beautiful pictures fill the pages and your juices can really start to flow. However, you can't do a good job without the proper tools. Here's a quick rundown of the tools that every meat lover's kitchen should have.

- Tongs are massively handy tools for the kitchen in general because, unless you have asbestos hands, they are essential for moving hot items of food around without burning your fingers.
- Carving forks are also useful when moving hot joints of meat and are vital for holding the meat still while carving.
- A good set of sharp knives makes all cutting easier and you are also less likely to do serious damage to yourself when cutting. A sharp knife is less likely to slip and less pressure is required to get the job done, so if you do slip you are

more likely to still have your fingers attached. However, you do get more little nicks and scratches as a result.

- A slide-out utility knife is the best readily available tool for scoring the fat on any meat for two main reasons. First, it is incredibly sharp, making scoring tough pork skin easy and giving a neater result; plus, at the first sign of blunting, the blade can be exchanged quickly and cheaply. Second, because the blade is extendable, you can set the length of the blade to how deeply you want to score the fat and get on with the job without worrying whether you have gone in too deep and damaged the flesh. I would strongly dissuade you from using a snap blade utility knife, because accidentally snapping the blade could lead to disastrous consequences.
- A good selection of pots, pans, roasting trays, and spoons is essential as well as self-explanatory.
- A temperature probe consists of a steel rod wired to a thermometer. When the probe is inserted into food, it tells you the internal temperature of whatever you are cooking (not only great for cooking all types of meat but also great for sugar products such as jams and caramels). This utensil is cheap and effective and allows you to ensure the meat is cooked properly for safe eating without having to overcook it to make sure. It's indispensable to home cooks and professional chefs alike. When buying a probe, opt for one with a metal wire attachment that enables the cable with prong to stay in the oven while the device sits outside during the cooking process so that constant monitoring is possible without continually opening the oven. Although I strongly recommend thermo-resistant wired digital thermometers, there are others on the market that do the same job for roasting but are not as accurate or versatile for other jobs and don't allow for constant monitoring of the contents of your oven.

- A nonwired digital instant-read probe is great for checking temperatures, but it will melt in the oven, so it won't allow for constant monitoring without opening and closing the oven.
- A temperature probe meat fork is a digital instant-read probe and a meat fork combined and is ideal for barbecues.
- An oven-safe dial probe is great for roasting because it can stay in the oven during cooking, and you can see the readout through the window of your oven door. However, because the readout is an average of the temperature along the entire probe, it cannot be used for thin cuts of meat, such as steaks and chops.
- Pop-up probes are only good for roasting joints, because they don't allow you to choose the level of doneness of your meat.

Now that you have an understanding of how to choose a pig, identify and select the correct cut, and ensure you have the right equipment for the job, it's time for the fun part: actually roasting the pig. Get ready to get those nostrils twitching . . .

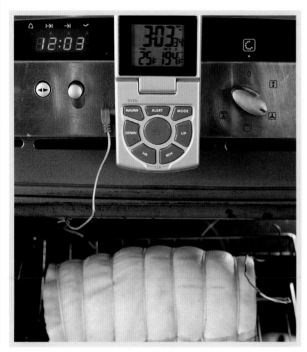

Using temperature probe

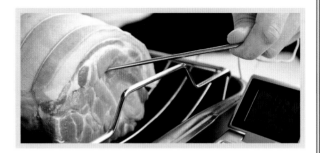

How to Use a Temperature Probe

To use a food thermometer correctly, place it in the center of the thickest part of the meat. It should not touch bone, fat, or gristle, because these conduct heat more quickly than does the meat itself. Start checking the temperature toward the end of cooking, but before you expect it to be done, checking the meat in several places to ensure that the meat is safe to eat through. Be sure to clean your food thermometer with hot soapy water before and after each use.

For more information on using a temperature probe, visit the USDA website:
http://www.fsis.usda.gov/Factsheets/Use_a_Food_Thermometer/index.asp

CHAPTER 2

Oven Roasting ★★★★★

Oven roasting is the most commonly used of all the roasting techniques, so it's the ideal place to start roasting pork to perfection. It's the go-to method when you are looking to feed five or more people with minimal effort and cooking time.

Due to the higher heat involved in the cooking process, the meat you select should be a reasonably tender cut with a good covering of fat to make sure it remains moist. Cuts of meat with these characteristics will give you the best results, but by altering the basic roasting method, good results can still be obtained from the slightly less tender cuts.

We'll start with a loin, because it is the easiest to get right and will generally provide the best results.

However, feel free to substitute another cut that is suited to oven roasting.

Which Joints Are Best?

Now that you understand the different parts of the pig and which methods to use with them, it's time to look at the best cuts to use, not in terms of price but in the quality that can be obtained from the finished product.

Finished loin of pork

LEG

Ease of roasting ★★★☆☆

Flavor ★★★★☆

Tenderness of end result ★★★☆☆

Quality of crackling ★★★☆☆

Cost ★★★★☆

The leg of pork (a.k.a. fresh ham) refers to the rear leg of the pig and also comes as smoked or cured hams. All three of these can be purchased both bone-in and boneless. This joint provides fantastic crackling (harder to get on ham but oh-so-good if you can get smoked crackling) and comes in a range of sizes, from a whole leg joint to smaller joints that are cut following individual muscles to reduce sinew in the meat. Oven roasting this joint is great for parties of up to twenty-five people all the way down to dinner for the family. However, larger joints will have a noticeable difference in thickness from one end to the other, which will mean one end cooks more rapidly than the other—something you simply have to accept as a trade-off for the lower price.

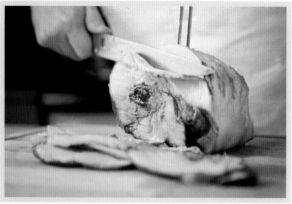

Roasted leg

PROS

- Okay crackling
- Great flavor
- Feeds four to twenty-five people
- Carves easily for larger parties (boneless)
- Good value

CONS

- Has a tendency to dry out quickly if overcooked
- Larger joints (serving twelve or more) will cook unevenly.

Butcher's Notes

The leg is a great all-around roasting joint, balancing good flavor and texture while still being moderately priced. The fact that it comes in three flavors—fresh, smoked, and cured—makes the leg an amazing culinary playground of flavors when deciding what to cook.

LOIN OF PORK

Ease of roasting ★★★★★

Flavor ★★★☆☆

Tenderness of end result ★★★★☆

Quality of crackling ★★★★★

Cost ★★☆☆☆

Roasted loin

The loin of pork is the king of the oven roasters and undoubtedly provides the best quality roast if cooked correctly. It is far less likely to dry out during cooking than the leg because it has a thick layer of back fat to melt through the meat and keep it moist. Like the leg, it is readily available both bone-in and boneless, but, due to the aforementioned back fat, the crackling yielded is far superior. It comes in a range of sizes, from a great family roaster to a whole loin of pork feeding upward of twenty-five people.

Loin cuts are fantastic for large roasts due to their uniformity in size. Loins also tend to be more uniform from pig to pig, preventing cooking times from differing greatly between the same size joint from different animals. This makes purchasing two loins a great option when feeding more people than one loin can serve.

PROS
- Amazing crackling
- Good flavor and soft in texture
- Feeds four to twenty-five people
- Carves easily for larger parties (boneless)
- Even fussy eaters will eat the succulent eye.

CONS
- One of the most expensive cuts of pork
- Less flavor than most other cuts

Butcher's Notes
The loin of pork is one of the most compact and uniform cuts of meat. If you have a small oven but are cooking for a large amount of people, this is a great option because, if laid out correctly (allowing for proper air movement in the oven), a boneless loin will yield the most amount of meat for your oven space of any pork cut.

TENDERLOIN

Ease of roasting ★★☆☆☆

Flavor ★★☆☆☆

Tenderness of end result ★★★★★

Quality of crackling N/A

Cost ★☆☆☆☆

Tenderloins are also taken from the loin area of the pork and are the pork equivalent to filet steak. Like its beef counterpart, tenderloin is the most expensive and tender cut of pork. Its mildness of flavor and lack of large deposits of fat and sinew (when trimmed properly) make it an ideal next step after chicken for those who don't eat much meat. The tenderloin is a long, thin muscle running down the inside of the spine, and a whole loin can feed eight to ten people. It is also characteristically very uniform between pigs, so it is easy to buy multiple loins if feeding more than eight people. It can also be roasted in one-person portions, so it makes a great "treat yourself" pork dinner.

PROS
- Very tender (even the fussiest of meat eaters will consume everything)
- Very lean, so great for people watching their fat intake

Roasted tenderloin

- Feeds anywhere from one to eight people (and you can fit multiple joints in your oven)
- Carves easily by just cutting medallions
- Is thin, so cooks and defrosts quickly

CONS
- Most expensive cut of pork
- Has no crackling and very little fat, so has a tendency to dry out very quickly

Butcher's Notes
Tenderloin is great to have in the freezer as an emergency, quick-defrost, elegant meal. The lack of crackling can be overcome by buying back fat separately to make crackling if, like me, you don't think that pork should be served without it. Tenderloins, because they have very little fat, tend to become a little dry during cooking, but this is easily prevented with an ingenious chef's trick (see page 141–144).

BOSTON BUTT

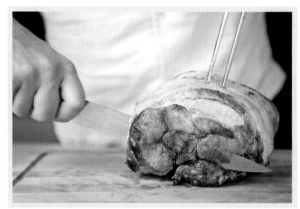

Ease of roasting ★★☆☆☆

Flavor ★★★★★

Tenderness of end result ★★★☆☆

Quality of crackling ★★★★☆

Cost ★★★★★

Despite its name, the Boston butt (a.k.a. shoulder roast, country roast, and blade roast) comes from the upper shoulder of the pig. It can be bought bone-in or boneless. Consisting of parts of the neck, shoulder blade, and upper arm, it is a cut with a lot of flavor, and, though it has a good deal of connective tissue and slightly tougher flesh, it is an amazing piece of meat to roast, brine, and marinate (see pages 146–147) it to help break down the connective tissue, which will leave it moister and more tender.

The full Boston butt is roughly the size of a soccer ball and weighs around 14 pounds (6.4 kg). It can be cut down into smaller joints, which are better for oven roasting, because when high-heat roasting, the full butt tends to be cooked on the outside long before the middle has reached a safe temperature. The makeup of the butt means that it is complex to carve neatly.

PROS
- Amazing flavor
- Well-distributed fat deposits (the joint is more forgiving to cook)

Roasted Boston butt

- Feeds four to thirty people
- Cheap roasting joint

CONS
- Larger roasts (for more than ten people) tend be overcooked on the outside by the time the interior is cooked
- Not great for fussy eaters
- Very difficult to carve neatly

Butcher's Notes
Boston butt is an amazing oven roast for family dinners and small gatherings, but anything larger should be cooked using a slow and low method. Buy it with the back fat attached because the 1½ inches (4 cm) of fat will help keep the meat moist while also offering up crackling. The combination of its slightly more flavorful meat and the great fat deposits make this the most flavorful of all the roasting joints.

Preparing Pork for Oven Roasting

And now the wait is over. Let's get started!

The first four steps are standard operating procedure when preparing any meat.

1. WASH THE MEAT

Rinse the entire surface of the meat under cold running water. This stage is important because when meat sits in packaging it will be marinating in its own blood and sweating. However, more important than rinsing the meat is ensuring that you do not splash the water from the meat onto work surfaces and utensils, and that the sink and its surroundings are sanitized properly afterward, because the pathogens that cause food poisoning can linger for days and remain on unsanitized surfaces for up to 48 hours.

2. DRY THE MEAT.

Pat the meat dry with paper towels. This prevents water from being absorbed, diluting the flavor and reducing the chance of the skin crackling properly.

3. REFRIGERATE THE MEAT.

Place the meat in the refrigerator for 30 minutes to an hour, allowing the air to circulate around it as much as possible. Use a cake cooling rack (set aside for meat only), placed on a baking tray (also reserved specifically for meat). This removes the last of the moisture from the surface of the meat and causes it to stiffen, making it easier to work with as you prep it.

4. MARINATE AND/OR BRINE THE MEAT.

If you are using a tougher cut of meat, marinating or brining is essential. If you wish to marinate or brine your meat, you should do it at this stage, following the process used to tenderize a Boston butt on pages 146–147. It is advisable to skip this step the first few times because it will complicate the process, plus you will struggle to get crackling.

Marinating pork imparts flavor and tenderizes the meat, while brining adds moisture and flavor and lightly tenderizes it. Doing both can work to great effect as long as the brining occurs first and you reduce the marinating time to no longer than 8 hours. Although doing both means that your preparation is going to take more than a day, it will leave you with a really tender, moist piece of meat, which is highly advisable if you

Scoring meat

Cross hatched scoring

wish to oven roast a tougher cut such as picnic or Boston butt.

5. SCORE THE CRACKLING.

If using a joint with skin for crackling, prepare it now. If not, skip to step 7.

Place the piece of meat on a secured chopping board and, using a sharp knife, score the skin and fat, getting as close to the flesh as possible without cutting into it. Make sure that, when the joint sits as it will be roasted, the slits are pointing straight down to enable the fat to exit the meat as quickly as possible and the slits run all the way to the end of the skin, thus allowing the excess fat to escape the joint without pooling at the bottom end. If your knife is very sharp, it is worth trying to score your crackling in a crisscross pattern.

Scoring the fat of the pork allows the fat and moisture trapped in the skin to escape quickly during cooking. Because the excess fat does not

remain under the skin, it cannot keep the skin and fat tissue moist. This means that the skin can blister and bubble and become crackling.

Conversely, the reason that you don't want to score through the fat into the flesh is that the remaining thin layer of fat acts as a barrier to the moisture from the pork flesh itself escaping through the fat and making the meat dry.

Crisscrossing the scoring pattern on the meat will ensure that more fat is rendered from the joint, so not only will your cracking look artistic, but it will also help your crackling be fantastically crisp and awesome.

SECURING A CHOPPING BOARD

All chopping boards you use should be secured to prevent them from slipping and greatly reducing the chance of injury. It also makes working much easier because your board will stay still. To secure a chopping board, take a clean cloth that is roughly the size of your chopping board, wet it, and place it underneath your board, ensuring that it is smooth and that your board won't rock.

Rubbed crackling

6. APPLY CRACKLING RUB.

For every area of crackling the size of the palm of an average human hand, mix ½ teaspoon salt and ½ teaspoon baking soda (bicarbonate of soda) together. Any type of salt will do, but sea or mineral salts are preferable because they will add another layer of flavoring to the meat and crackling while seasoning it. Baking soda draws the moisture out of the skin like salt does.

HANDY HINT

Baking soda is a great way to lower your salt intake. You can replace all the salt if you wish to reduce your sodium intake, although your meat will not be seasoned.

Using one hand, open the slits you have made in the skin of the pork and sprinkle a generous amount of salt mix into the openings. Repeat this with every one of the incisions you have made in the pork. Lightly dust the rest of the pork with plain salt and return to the fridge for up to 24 hours, ensuring that the pork is raised up out of the tray to prevent it from sitting in the salty brine that will pool at the bottom of the container. When you are ready to move on, repeat steps 1 to 3 above to remove the salt from the surface of the pork.

The reason for salting the crackling is to allow the process called osmosis to draw out as much of the moisture from the fat tissue. This reduction in moisture really makes a difference in the quality of your cracking. The longer you leave the salt on, the more moisture will leave the fat, and the crisper the crackling will be. You need to find the correct balance for your palate yourself, because the longer you leave the salt on, the better the crackling will be but also the saltier it will become.

A great way to add a little extra flavor is to try adding herbs or spices to the salt/baking soda mix. I like to add Cajun spices or dried sage, but get experimental—any dry flavoring you can think of will work as long as there is no sugar in it.

HANDY HINT

If you are short on time and only have a couple of hours to salt the joint, you can use a bit more salt and baking soda mix on the meat to speed the process, but it won't yield as good a result as giving the process time.

Cooking loin roast in the oven

7. SEASON THE MEAT.

Now, all that is left to do is season the meat with only salt, sprinkling it to taste all over the meat, including the crackling.

Seasoning is important because it not only adds flavor but also intensifies and brings out the flavors in meat. When using the basic method, you should not use any other spice, including pepper, because it will burn during the sealing process and impart an acrid taste to your meat.

Cooking the Meat

Now the meat starts to dictate the pace at which you progress. As such, I won't give you specific timings for cooking the meat because it will only be ready when it is ready, not when an allotted time has expired. However, as a general guide, allow for 10 minutes plus:

- 30 minutes per pound for thinner cuts (distance to the core of the cut less than 2 inches [5 cm]), such as loin and small ham roasts

- 35 minutes per pound for thicker cuts (distance to the core of the cut more than 2 inches [5 cm]), such as Boston butt and whole leg roasts

Sealing meat

> ## HANDY HINT
>
> Sealing the meat will require a pan large enough to comfortably fit the entire joint. Ideally, use a nonstick, thick-bottomed frying pan, but for larger joints the roasting pan will do.

While the oven is still cool, remove everything (except the shelves) to enable efficient airflow in the oven, which helps ensure an even cooking temperature.

Arrange the shelves to ensure that you can fit everything into the oven quickly and easily so that you avoid burns and have the oven open for as short a time as possible, keeping the heat at a more steady temperature.

Preheat the oven to 480°F (240°C, or gas mark 9). Allowing your oven to preheat is essential to the roasting process, because having a nice high heat to start with will help render off more fat in the early stages of cooking, before you turn down the temperature to that at which you will finish the cooking.

1. SEAL THE MEAT.

Lightly oil and preheat a frying pan. You are ready to start sealing as soon as you see the first signs of the oil starting to smoke. Sealing the meat is a simple process that involves browning all the flesh of the meat (but not the fat and skin if you want crackling). Using your tongs, place the meat in the pan. Don't move it for 30 seconds to a minute, which allows it time to brown. Lift the meat and place it back in the pan to brown another section. Repeat this until all the surface of the flesh has been lightly browned, allowing the temperature of the pan to rise back up for each additional piece of meat.

Sealing is important, because the browning process (called the Maillard reaction) is essential for flavor, because this is where the distinctive roast meat flavors are produced.

2. PREPARE THE ROASTING PAN.

While you are sealing the meat, prepare a roasting tray with trivets. Trivets' primary role is to lift the meat off the roasting tray so that you are not frying the meat on the metal base of the pan, causing it to dry out. It also allows air to flow around the joint to promote even cooking.

There are two types of trivets available: metal racks or natural ones, such as bones and vegetables.

For metal trivets, simply lay them in the bottom of the pan and you are ready. It's that simple.

Natural trivets

Natural trivets consist of traditional stock vegetables (onions, carrots, and celery) and/or bones. Cut the onions in half through the middle, peel the carrots (if they are wider than a hot dog, cut them in half through the middle as well), and cut the celery into sticks roughly the size of the carrots. Bones, if you are adding them, should be prepared in advance by your butcher, who is equipped to do so quickly, safely, and easily.

When you have prepared your trivets, put them into the roasting pan, add a drizzle of oil, and toss (like a salad) to ensure that everything gets an even coating of oil. Spread out the trivets to ensure that the meat will lay flat in the tray while leaving space for airflow around the joint.

Even though metal trivets are more effective at ensuring more even roasting due to better airflow around the meat, natural ones add color and, more important, flavor to your gravy.

THE SCIENCE OF THE MAILLARD REACTION

The Maillard reaction is the scientific name for the chemical changes that occur during the browning process in certain types of food. This happens because once the proteins in the meat hit 284°F (140°C), the proteins and carbohydrates react together to produce new chemical combinations that make that amazing roast smell and flavor in meat. This reaction takes place in many foods, not just meats, and is what causes the browning of potatoes and the crust of brioche, to name just two.

3. INSERT THE PROBE AND PLACE THE PAN IN THE OVEN.

Place the pork on the trivets and insert a temperature probe (if you have one that can be used while in the oven), ensuring that the tip is in the center of the meat but away from bone. The probe needs to be in the center of the meat because this is where the heat takes longest to reach, so this will be the last part of the meat to reach a safe temperature. The probe tip also needs to be away from bone because bone heats up and conducts heat quicker than meat does, meaning that the meat will heat up quicker next to bone and give you a false reading on your probe. Place the pan in the oven.

4. HOT FLASH THE MEAT.

For the first 10 minutes of cooking time, have the oven really hot—480°F (240°C, or gas mark 9)—before lowering the heat. This intense heat continues the browning Maillard reaction that gives you the fantastic roast meat flavor. It also starts the fat in the soon-to-be crackling (if present on your joint) melting quickly, giving your crackling a really good head start.

5. LOWER THE TEMPERATURE AND COOK THE MEAT.

After the hot flash, lower the temperature of the oven to 280°F (140°C, or gas mark 1) for the rest of the cooking process until the core temperature of the pork reaches 145°F (63°C).

Finished roast ready to carve

This may seem like a rather low roasting temperature, but it really works this way. In a conventional "how to roast" recipe, the browning reaction happens slowly throughout the cooking process. But by sealing the meat, then hot flashing it, you have created most of those lovely roast flavors in the first part of the cooking process; now you just cook the meat through. This lower roasting temperature means that:

- The meat heats more evenly throughout the joint, resulting in moist, succulent meat all the way through.
- More of the connective tissue is broken down, leaving the meat more tender.
- The proteins in the meat shrink less, so less juice is squeezed from the meat, leaving the joint much more tender.
- The roast takes a little longer to cook.

TROUBLESHOOTING

PROBLEM: The meat is starting to burn on the outside before the core temperature has reached 145°F (63°C).

SOLUTION: Lower the temperature to 150°F (65°C) and finish cooking the joint slowly.

PROBLEM: The trivets are starting to burn.

SOLUTION: Remove the pork from the oven and douse the trivets with chicken stock, using a wooden spoon to deglaze all the caramelized juices from the bottom of the roasting tin. Add enough stock to cool the trivets but not fill the bottom of the pan, then replace the pork and return to the oven to finish roasting.

PROBLEM: The crackling is starting to burn.

SOLUTION: Remove the pork from the oven, pull the crackling away from the meat, and set it aside to be served when the pork is done. This is best done with tongs (to avoid burned fingers) and is quite simple because the fat tissue has melted and become soft and no longer has much of a hold on the crackling.

PROBLEM: The skin is not crackling properly.

SOLUTION: Fear not, intrepid roasters, your worst nightmare is easily solved.

As with burned crackling, you're going to need to remove the skin to enable you to artificially crackle it under the grill. This is a little trickier than removing crackling because the fat tissue is, most likely, relatively intact, but with the help of a sharp knife it is still easily removed. Once off, place it flat on a baking sheet and finish it off under a medium broiler, ensuring that the crackling is about 5 inches (12.7 cm) from the heat source. You really need to keep an eye on the crackling because it will crackle very suddenly, then start to burn. This problem is a good indicator that you didn't put enough salt on the skin or leave it there for long enough to ensure sufficient drying.

6. REMOVE THE PORK FROM THE OVEN.
Once the core temperature of the pork has reached 145°F (63°C), remove the pork from the oven.

If you roast your meat to 145°F (63°C), the temperature will continue to rise by 5° to 10°F (2° to 4°C) after you remove the meat from the oven, leaving you with meat that is moist and juicy with a very faint tinge of pink. DON'T BE ALARMED. The U.S. Department of Agriculture (USDA) states that pork need only be cooked over 145°F (63°C) to ensure that it is safe to eat, and yours will end up 5°F (2°C) higher, so your meat is more than safe to eat. The myth that you have to cook pork really well to make it safe to eat dates back to the time before temperature probes were widely available. With a temperature probe, you can now throw away the better-safe- (and overcooked) than-sorry approach and embrace cooking pork to perfection.

Serving the Pork

By now, the ravening hordes will be beating at the door to get into the kitchen like zombies crazed with the lust for flesh. But they must wait awhile; they may be able to see the pork, but it's not quite ready to eat yet.

1. LET THE MEAT REST.

Remove the meat from the roasting tray and put it in the warmest place in your kitchen. Cover with a clean oven cloth (tinfoil will do, but because it doesn't breathe, condensation may ruin your crackling) and allow it to rest before carving.

Resting time is important, yet to most people it's a mystery, and I'm not going to tell you why because it's complex and rather dull. You're just going to have to trust me and accept that it's important and will result in more tender and juicy meat that is also much easier to carve.

If you're looking for perfection, rest the meat until it cools to 120°F (50°C). With most joints this works out to be roughly 8 minutes per pound, so it can be a rather long time. For people who can't wait this long, leave roasted joints for 20 minutes at the bare minimum. Resting has the upside of allowing you plenty of time to get the rest of the meal together knowing that your meat is perfect and you don't have to worry about it. Plus the crackling is ready, so it's only polite to take the chef's prerogative and test for quality control a bit (or in my case, as much as I can get away with).

CARVING BASICS

The first essential is a long-bladed, sharp carving knife. Use the knife with a long gentle sawing movement so that it passes smoothly through the meat. Using long strokes of the knife ensures the knife is changing direction less, resulting in less tearing of the meat and better carving.

Use a carving fork fitted with a guard to protect your hand.

Carve the joint firmly on a large warmed dish. A wooden board can be used but a bespoke carving dish is preferable; spiked dishes are particularly good for holding the joint firmly in place and preventing it from slipping as you carve. Boards or dishes with gullies will catch the meat juices, which can be added to the gravy.

Whenever possible, carve across the grain of the meat, thus shortening the fibers so the meat gives the illusion of being more tender. The grain is easy to spot because it's the direction of the string-like fibers of the muscle. Whenever possible, make your cuts perpendicular to the direction in which the fibers lay to make the most of your meat.

2. CARVE THE MEAT.

Thinly slice the meat and transfer to a warmed plate. When you've finished carving, pour a little of the gravy over the meat to add a little more heat and moisture. Divide up the crackling and serve.

Good carving is a skill worth learning, because it makes a joint go much further than merely hacking off the meat. By allowing the meat to

Roasted Boston butt

Boston butt in brine

rest, you make it firmer and easier to carve more evenly. This will help you maximize the portions you get from your meat.

Ideally, before you progress to experimenting with oven roasting or move on to slow roasting after this section, you should have roasted a couple of joints so that you get a perfect roast every time. Once you've mastered the basic technique, move on to playing with your food.

Experimenting with Your Food

In this section we'll explore two ways of taking your roasts to the next level: tenderizing a Boston butt by brining and marinating it, and packing flavor into a loin of pork with a Cajun marinade and spice rub.

Tenderizing a Boston Butt

Boston butt is in the category of oven roasting with one caveat: marinate and brine the meat, or it will be a little tough and chewy. This method works for all cuts of meat, making less tender joints suitable for oven roasting and tender joints juicier than ever before.

This example uses a Boston butt that has been boned, rolled, and had its skin removed. This is because the fat will absorb plenty of liquid during the brining process, making the skin almost

Marinated meat

impossible to crackle. Reserve the skin to make crackling under the broiler (see page 141).

INGREDIENTS

Boston butt of desired size, boned, rolled, and skin removed and reserved

Brine of your choice (page 147)

Marinade of your choice (page 146)

1. WASH, DRY, AND REFRIGERATE THE MEAT UNTIL READY TO USE.

See page 34.

2. BRINE THE MEAT.

Using a pot big enough for the meat to sit in comfortably, mix enough brine to cover the meat in its entirety. Place the meat in the brine and leave it for up to 24 hours in the refrigerator, then remove and pat dry with paper towels.

3. MARINATE THE MEAT.

Place the meat in a plastic bag large enough to fit comfortably and add enough marinade of your choice to fill the bottom 2 inches (5 cm) of the bag. Squeeze out excess air so that the marinade covers the meat and refrigerate for 5 to 8 hours; then remove and pat dry with paper towels.

4. SEASON THE MEAT.

Because the brining process already seasons the meat, reduce the amount of salt you would usually use to season your meat by half.

5. SEAL THE MEAT.

See page 38.

Finished Cajun roasted pork

6. HOT FLASH THE MEAT.

See page 40.

7. COOK THE MEAT.

See page 40. The crackling will probably be ready before the meat, so remove this when it is done.

8. LET THE MEAT REST.

Carve and serve with whatever crackling you haven't already eaten.

Packing in the Flavor: Cajun Pork

With this variation, we are going to go back to the loin of pork, but this time we are going to alter the basic method and really pack in the flavor using a Cajun spice rub to bring some Southern flair into your kitchen. You can use any spice rub you like,

Wrapped Cajun marinated loin

either store-bought or homemade (see page 144 for recipes). You can apply this technique to any tender cut of meat you wish.

The loin of pork is marinated with a Cajun marinade to tenderize and allow the flavors to permeate deep into the meat, then finished with a spice rub to add a crust of intense flavor.

INGREDIENTS

Loin of pork of desired size

Cajun rub (page 145)

White wine vinegar of cider vinegar

Dijon mustard

1. WASH, DRY, AND REFRIGERATE THE MEAT UNTIL READY TO USE.

See page 34

2. MARINATE THE MEAT.

Mix the Cajun rub with a splash of white wine vinegar or cider vinegar (to form a paste), cover all the meat except the crackling with a thick layer and wrap the meat in plastic wrap; as you wrap the meat, squeeze a little of the marinating rub onto the skin. Place in the fridge skin side up and marinate for up to 12 hours. When ready to continue, remove the plastic wrap, then wash and pat the meat dry with paper towels to remove any surface liquid.

The acid in the vinegar helps the flavors of the rub permeate into the meat much more quickly, due to the acid's effect on the meat proteins. This trick turns any rub into a thick marinade that will not slosh around, and it will pack in more flavor but will tenderize less compared to a wet marinade.

Cajun pork

3. SCORE THE CRACKLING.

See page 35.

4. APPLY CRACKLING RUB.

This is the same as on page 36, but add ½ teaspoon Cajun rub per 1 teaspoon salt in the crackling rub. This will bring another dimension to your crackling that will really complement the flavor imparted to the meat.

Place in the fridge and allow the rub do its magic for up to 24 hours. When you remove the pork, wash and dry the meat (see page 34) before moving on.

5. SEAL THE MEAT.

See page 38.

6. APPLY THE SPICE RUB.

Using a pastry brush, paint a thin layer of Dijon mustard onto the meat, avoiding the skin for the crackling. Sprinkle a generous dusting of the Cajun rub over the mustard. The mustard will not be a dominant flavor and is purely here to act as glue for the spices to stick to. If you are using a rub that will clash with the little mustard flavor there is, skip the sealing stage and just rub your spices into the meat directly. Otherwise, you will find it hard to make the spices stick to sealed meat, and if you seal the meat afterward you will burn the spices, ruining their flavor. To boost the natural roast flavor, simply add another 5 minutes to the hot flash stage to allow the Maillard reaction to occur.

7. HOT FLASH THE MEAT

See page 40.

8. COOK THE MEAT

See page 40.

9. LET THE MEAT REST, THEN CARVE AND SERVE.

Signature Dish: Pork Tenderloin

Now you're ready to oven roast like a pro, so I'm going to give you one of my signature dishes utilizing a sneaky trick that makes the "prone to dryness" tenderloin one of the easiest cuts of meat to cook while resulting in a really classy-looking dish.

INGREDIENTS
Pork tenderloin
Whole-grain mustard
1 slice Prosciutto or Parma ham (any air-dried ham will do) for every 2 inches (5 cm) of tenderloin
Small bunch young, tender sage, stalks removed

1. WASH, DRY, AND REFRIGERATE THE MEAT UNTIL READY TO USE.
See page 34.

2. APPLY EXTRA FLAVOR.
Coat the tenderloin with a thin layer of whole-grain mustard and place the meat on one side. Make sure you have enough space to place the entire loin on your work surface. Lay out a layer of plastic wrap with roughly 3 inches (7.5 cm) of excess wrap on each side of the tenderloin. Add a second layer of plastic wrap over the first exactly the same size and rub with a tea towel to get the two layers of wrap to stick together.

3. PLACE THE HAM ON THE PLASTIC WRAP.
Overlapping each slice by about ¼ inch (6 mm) to create a sheet of ham. Place a line of sage leaves 1 inch (2.5 cm) from the closest edge of the layer of ham. Place the tenderloin on the sage leaves.

4. WRAP IT UP.
Grab the closest edge of plastic wrap and lift it so that the inch (2.5 cm) of ham closest to you wraps smoothly around the tenderloin.

5. ROLL THE TENDERLOIN INTO THE REST OF THE HAM.
So that you end up with the ham completely encasing the meat. Don't wrap the meat too tightly

...Parma ham laid on plastic wrap

3. Laying on sage leaves

5. Tenderloin first fold

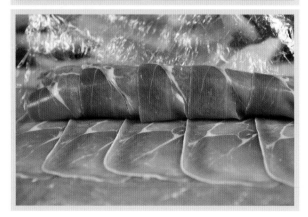

6. Sealed wrapped tenderloin

8. Tenderloin cooking

because the ham will shrink during sealing and squeeze moisture from the meat.

Fold back the plastic wrap and leave it flat on the kitchen counter. You will be coming back to this later.

Place the meat in the fridge for 15 to 20 minutes. This will cause all the components to stick together better and make the following steps easier.

6. SEAL THE MEAT.

Unroll the meat from the plastic wrap. Place the meat in a preheated nonstick pan over medium-high heat. If you don't have a big enough pan, cut the meat down until it will fit. Drizzle the pan with oil and seal the meat all over, allowing the ham to brown gently. The ham should now have shrunk enough to snugly wrap the meat in the center of the roll. Place the meat back on the plastic wrap and allow it to cool for 5 to 10 minutes. Skipping the cooling will cause the meat to sweat once it is wrapped up again.

7. REWRAP THE MEAT.

Once the meat has cooled, bring it to the near side of the plastic wrap and wrap the whole piece of meat up again. This needs to be done so that the wrap fits snugly around the meat, making a tight cylinder. Now twist the ends of the wrap to tighten and make a seal.

Grab some aluminum foil and lay out two sheets the same way you did with the plastic wrap, then tightly roll the rolled meat in these two layers. The double layer of plastic wrap will help hold the meat in shape, giving you perfectly circular medallions while also helping the meat retain a lot of moisture during cooking. The aluminum foil around the outside of the wrap prevents the plastic from burning. This makes it almost impossible to dry out tenderloins (or other meats you use this method with) ever again.

8. COOK THE MEAT.

Preheat the oven to 150°F (65°C) and place the rolled and wrapped meat on metal trivets to promote even airflow around it. Place in the oven to cook.

An average tenderloin is roughly ⅔ inch (1.7 cm) thick and should take about 30 to 35 minutes to reach a core temperature of the desired 145°F (63°C).

This is the really clever bit. Because tenderloins have very little connective tissue that needs breaking down, there is no need to set your oven over the temperature at which collagen breaks down (160° to 170°F [70° to 75°C]). By setting the oven to the desired core temperature of the meat there is no chance of overcooking the meat, and your meat could technically be left in the oven for prolonged periods without causing much degradation to the quality. However, you have to be able to make sure

CHEF'S TIPS

This low-heat principle can be applied to all of the really tender cuts of meat that are purely muscle, such as the eye of the loin. This method of having your cooking medium (usually using the air in an oven or the water in a bain-marie) set to the ideal temperature of your meat is the way that a lot of the top chefs produce perfectly cooked meat every time.

that your oven is reaching 150°F (65°C) or you will be waiting forever for your meat to cook. This is another great thing about oven thermometers, because not only can you check the internal temperatures of the meat in the oven as it cooks but you can also accurately check the temperature of the oven. If you don't have an oven thermometer you should raise the oven temperature to 155°F (70°C) just to make sure.

9. LET THE MEAT REST.

Once the meat has reached the desired core temperature, remove it from the oven and allow it to rest without removing the wrapping. This means any juice that has escaped will be held around the meat as it relaxes and some will be reabsorbed, making it extra juicy.

10. OPEN THE PACKET.

Be careful when opening the packet because, at this point, it is easy to rip the ham from the meat and spoil the presentation of your dish. The best way I have found is to cut off one end of the packet and slide a small but sharp paring knife inside, then cut it open away from the meat.

11. CARVE THE MEAT.

Using a very sharp knife, carve the meat into medallions and serve.

Now that you have a thorough understanding of oven roasting pork, it's time to slow things down a little. Get ready to delve into the realm of melting slow roasts and meaty terrines, and experience the magical delights of pulled pork. If the words alone don't make your mouth water, you've never tasted it cooked properly. Get ready for one of the best things you've ever put in your mouth.

Plated Pork Tenderloin

CHAPTER 3

Slow Roasting ★★★★★

Slow roasting is a fantastically versatile cooking method that can be applied to almost all cuts of pork while still getting good results. Along with pot roasting, this is the best method to use when the time of serving is likely to vary. It also turns some of the cheapest cuts into the best-tasting melt-in-your-mouth pork you will ever taste.

The basic rule of slow cooking is the longer you cook it, the more tender the meat will be, and as long as it has plenty of fat, the meat will stay moist as well. Slow cooking allows you to utilize the more flavorful but tougher (and cheaper) cuts, making this the best method to use if you really want a natural and intense roast pork flavor. It's also the method to use if you are making what is undoubtedly my favorite sandwich filler of the summer: pulled pork.

Which Joints Are Best?

When looking for the perfect joint to slow roast, choose one with a good covering of fat on the outside of the meat as well as a good deal of marbling throughout the joint to prevent the meat from drying out. The reason that the cheaper cuts of meat are so great for this method is their comparatively high fat content. This acts as a moisturizer for the meat as it melts during the cooking process while also adding to the rich meaty taste of your pork.

This melting fat is what makes it possible to cook the meat long enough to allow the temperature to gently rise to 172°F (78°C) without drying out. At about this temperature the connective tissues made of collagen (which is pound-for-pound stronger than steel) becomes water-soluble gelatin that slowly dissolves (hydrolyzes). This hydrolization of the collagen doesn't happen all at once but as soon as the meat gets to temperature. It takes time, meaning that the meat has finished cooking when you decide it is tender enough. And if you get it right you will end up with lubricious, tender meat that is, oh-so palate-pleasing.

Dressed shoulder

BELLY

Ease of roasting ★★★★☆

Flavor ★★★★★

Tenderness of end result ★★★★★

Quality of crackling ★★★★★

Cost ★★★★★

The belly is taken from the side of the pig and is the part that streaky bacon is made from. As you know from looking at streaky bacon it is made up of multiple thin layers of meat and fat with a layer of skin on one side. Unlike other fattier cuts of pork, this is not a heavily worked set of muscles and so has little tough connective tissue in the meat. These characteristics make pork belly an amazingly tender and moist piece of meat when cooked correctly or a greasy, chewy monstrosity if done badly (which, if slow roasted, is really hard to do).

PROS
- Amazing flavor (possibly the most flavorful cut of the pig)
- Really forgiving to cook with
- Feeds twenty-five people
- Great crackling
- Pound for dollar one of the cheapest cuts of meat on the pig

CONS
- The thin layering of meat and fat means fussy eaters who only eat flesh will be picking through their pork for hours
- Not the greatest cut of meat if you are looking to control your calorie or fat intake
- If not allowed to rest, will fall to pieces when carving

PORK BELLY

In the United States the belly is almost always used for bacon. In other parts of the world bacon is made from other parts of the animal, back, and side. In Central America and the United States, if you ask for bacon, you will get streaky bacon (as it's known in the United Kingdom), or slice/strip, as it's called in the United States. It is possible to get a whole cured belly-bacon joint, which is a real treat for roasting. It's way more expensive than a fresh belly but is worth trying to find.

Roasted belly

Butcher's Notes

Belly is my favorite cut of meat from the whole pig, and slow roasted is the best way to prepare it. The thin layers of meat in a well-cooked belly are as moist and tender as those of the tenderloin. The layers of fat in between the meat are ideally situated to keep the roast moist and add flavor as it renders out (shrinking the fat layer massively in the process) while being able to escape the meat easily enough, leaving soft, tasty layers of fat layered with tender meat. It's got a great layer of fat under the skin to help the crackling really crisp up, but the fat in between the muscle escapes easily, leaving amazing crackling. And it's one of the cheapest cuts of the pig.

Pork belly can also be roasted quickly with good results if the meat has come from a lean pig (fat layers less than ¼-inch [6 mm] wide), but buying a piece of pork with a good covering of fat (almost all heritage breeds) and taking the time to prep it and then slow roast it really leaves you with something truly special and very worth your while.

BOSTON BUTT

Ease of roasting ★★★★★

Flavor ★★★★★

Tenderness of end result ★★★★☆

Quality of crackling ★★★☆☆

Cost ★★☆☆☆

Roasted Boston butt

A full Boston butt is roughly the size of a soccer ball, weighs around 14 pounds (6.4 kg), and can feed up to thirty people. When looking for a butt to slow roast, buy one with the layer of back fat still attached, because this will melt through the joint, keeping the meat extra moist. This is the joint that also makes the best pulled pork when slow roasted; it's a great way to have a hog roast–style meal without having to roast a whole pig.

PROS

- Great, rich, intense meaty flavor
- Used for making pulled pork
- Feeds four to thirty people
- Reasonably cheap roasting joint

CONS

- Large round joint takes up a large amount of oven space for the yielded portions
- Large joints can take a long time to cook
- Not all joints will have skin to crackle

Butcher's Notes

The Boston butt made its way into the oven-roasting section as well as this one because it not only is a great piece of meat but, unlike with oven roasting, you can still get great results from large joints when you slow roast. In fact, the larger the joint, the better the roast tends to be with slow roasting. The flesh is a slightly darker color than that from the loin. It has a richer, meatier flavor and a great fat deposit but a good deal of connective tissue. Slow roasting a Boston butt means more time for the connective tissue to break down than with oven roasting.

PICNIC

Ease of roasting ★★★★★

Flavor ★★★★★

Tenderness of end result ★★★★☆

Quality of crackling ★★☆☆☆

Cost ★★★★☆

Roasted picnic

The picnic cut (a.k.a. hand of pork) is a fantastic slow-roasting joint comprising the lower part of the shoulder of the pig and including the top part of the foreleg. This joint is available on or off the bone. This is very similar to the Boston butt (the top part of the shoulder) but is a lot smaller, with a full bone-in shoulder only weighing 9 to 10 pounds (4 to 4.5 kg) and feeding up to twenty-five people. It is a flavorful and moist joint that has a lot of connective tissue; this is what makes the picnic cut a slow and low joint only, but it is a fantastic one. The joint is both slightly richer and has meatier flesh and better fat deposits than a butt does, making it a great cheaper, more flavorful alternative to Boston butt.

PROS
- Great rich, intense meaty flavor
- Used for making pulled pork
- Feeds four to twenty-five people
- Low-cost joint

CONS
- Not great for fussy eaters, because even with slow roasting some connective tissue will still be present
- Very difficult to carve when bone-in because it gets in the way; boneless is still quite difficult to carve because it is has a tendency to fall apart.

Butcher's Notes
The picnic cut is a very flavorful piece of meat with great texture. It has probably the highest amount of collagen in the pig and needs the longest cooking of all to fully tenderize. Once you have cooked this meat low and slow, you will see just how good tough meat can become.

HOCKS AND SHANKS

Ease of roasting ★★★★☆

Flavor ★★★★★

Tenderness of end result ★★★☆☆

Quality of crackling ★★★☆☆

Cost ★★★★☆

Hocks are the lower part of the leg and shoulder joints: with the skin and fat left on them they make fantastic mini roasting joints. They are also widely available as the by-products of hams (called bacon joints) and are available cured or smoked, making them an amazingly versatile cheap cut. Although there is a lot of connective tissue in the meat, these joints are packed with flavor and benefit from being both well marbled with fat and on the bone. Slow roasting breaks down the connective tissue, making the meat tender while the fat that completely surrounds the meat melts through the flesh, leaving amazingly flavored and moist meat. Due to their size, the shanks are great for single-person mini roasts and the hocks are great for two-person dinners.

PROS
- Good meaty flavor
- Really cheap cut
- Feeds one or two
- Smoked hocks and shanks make smoked crackling.

Roasted shank

CONS
- The large bone running through the middle of the meat can be off-putting to the fussier eater.
- Meat from cured ham is hard to crackle and sometimes slightly gelatinous.

Butcher's Notes

When it comes to hocks and shanks, make some smoked ham crackling as soon as you can. It's very hard to make ham crackle naturally, but you can crackle the skin artificially under a broiler set to medium heat while the joint is resting.

Hocks and shanks make lovely little roasts for one or two people. Serving shanks as an individual portion is a great dinner-party idea because each person has their own mini roast pork joint, which you don't have to carve. Don't attempt this for more than ten or twelve guests—shanks and hocks take up a lot of oven space for the number of portions yielded.

Salt and baking soda applied to scores

Preparing Pork for Slow Roasting

Preparing pork for slow roasting is very similar to preparing it for oven roasting, so the standard operating procedures (steps 1 through 4 on page 34).

Almost all slow-roasting joints have skin to crackle on them, but if you are roasting with the skin off, skip to step 7.

5. SCORE THE CRACKLING.

Firmly secure the meat on a chopping board in the manner that you intend the meat to sit in the oven. With a sharp knife, score the skin as deep as the fat goes without cutting into the flesh itself. Score the skin in one direction only, making sure that the incision is made all the way from one end of the crackling to the other to allow a gully for the fat to escape from during the cooking process. Make incisions parallel to the first every ¼ inch (6 mm) until the whole skin is scored.

Unlike with oven roasting, it is not desirable to use the crisscross scoring pattern on the skin in most cases. This is because the meat has a longer cooking time, so more fat will melt away and run through the meat, and if all the fat melts the meat will start to dry out. For this reason, crisscross scoring should be reserved for joints that have a large amount of fat on them (more than a ¾-inch [2 cm] layer and up) because these will not dry out, and they will need the extra rendering to make the fat palatable and the skin crackle.

6. RUB THE CRACKLING.

Using a mixture of ½ teaspoon salt and ½ teaspoon baking soda per hand of surface area (see page 36), rub the crackling, ensuring you push the mix into every one of the scores in the skin. Then lightly season the flesh part of the meat with salt and return it to the fridge, ensuring that the meat is raised from the bottom of the tray (a cooling rack works well), and leave for 24 hours if possible. When ready to cook the meat, wash and dry the meat (see page 34) and then move on to the next step.

This process is exactly the same as when oven roasting, and it has the same effect of drawing moisture from the fat to make the skin of the pork crackle.

FLAVOR BOOST

As with oven roasting, flavors can be added to the rub and the salt can be substituted by doubling the amount of baking soda.

7. SEASON THE MEAT.

Finally, season the meat with a generous coating of salt but lightly season the crackling because the previous rub of salt and baking soda will have seasoned the skin.

Cooking the Meat

The main differences between slow raosting and oven roasting are the temperature the meat is cooked at and the length of time that it cooks for. The temperature you will roast your meat at is set at 170°F (75°C), because at this temperature all the forms of collagen in the meat will start to turn to gelatin. However, the length of time that the meat requires will vary and should be judged as ready when the meat no longer feels springy or tough to the touch. This should take 30 minutes plus:

- 35 minutes per pound for thinner cuts (distance to the core of the meat less than 2 inches [5 cm])
- 40 minutes per pound for thicker cuts (distance to the core more than 2 inches [5 cm])

Ensure you have removed all excess trays from the oven to promote even airflow, and preheat the oven to 475°F (245°C, or gas mark 9) or its highest temperature.

1. SEAL THE MEAT.

Over high heat, heat a lightly oiled pan big enough for the meat to sit in (preferably thick bottomed and nonstick) until you see the first sign of smoke from the oil. Gently lay the meat in the pan and allow to brown (roughly 30 seconds to a minute depending on the pan you use) before turning

1. Sealing the shoulder

the meat to another side to brown. Repeat until the entire surface is browned. Once all the meat is browned, turn the heat down to medium-high and pour any surface fat in the pan away. Place the meat back in the pan, this time with the skin side down, and leave for about a minute to allow the crackling to take on a slightly sandy texture but not start to brown.

CHEF'S TIP

With slow roasting, you seal the crackling as well as the meat to give it a head start, because in the oven it will have less heat to continue the crackling process after the hot flash.

If after a minute or so the skin has not started to take on the sandy texture, pour the fat that has rendered from the pork away and return the pan to the heat again. The reason that you don't oil the pan is that you are looking to sear and scorch the skin so that it starts to blister: any form of fat will prevent the skin from blistering and will fry it instead, making your crackling denser and harder.

2. PREPARE THE ROASTING PAN.
See page 39.

3. INSERT THE PROBE AND PLACE THE PAN IN THE OVEN.
See page 40.

4. HOT FLASH THE MEAT.
Place the meat in the preheated oven for at least 10 minutes before reducing the temperature.

5. Shoulder in the oven

WHERE TO PLACE THE MEAT IN THE OVEN

When it comes to placing a roasting joint in the oven, as long as you have a fan-assisted oven, it really doesn't matter where it goes. However, if you have a gas oven without a fan, the meat should be placed on a shelf, leaving the center of the meat as close to the middle of the oven as possible and as close to the door without touching it. This is because the center of the oven tends to have the most even temperature and thus provides more even cooking. The joint is placed at the front of the shelf because gas ovens heat from the back: moving the joint forward removes it from direct heat and keeps it from over-browning or burning.

You may find the crackling gets too brown or even burned around the edges. This happens when you have over-sealed the crackling: once when you were sealing the meat and then when you sealed the crackling. This is fixable: Once the hot flash is over, remove the meat from the pan, place it on a chopping board, and use the back of a knife to scrape the charred pieces away. Leaving this on at this stage will allow the flavor to permeate into the meat and crackling, leaving it with a burned taste. But don't scrape it while it is still in the roasting pan, because this will ruin your gravy.

5. LOWER THE TEMPERATURE AND COOK THE MEAT
After the hot flash, lower the temperature to 170°F (75°C) and continue cooking the meat until the core temperature has reached 170°F (75°C).

It's really hard to overcook slow-roasted pork with this method; even though it is a long cooking time, the temperature is so low that it can't do much damage to the meat tissue.

As with my oven-roasting technique, the actual cooking temperature is really much lower than your standard roasting guide and is set to the temperature your meat needs to reach to become tender without applying excess heat and causing the external meat to dry out too much. This is the most utilitarian way of cooking because you can prepare the joint at lunchtime (or breakfast if the joint has a good amount of fat on it), put it in the oven, and forget about it until dinner.

6. REMOVE THE PORK FROM THE OVEN.

Once the meat has reached a core temperature of 170°F (75°C), the meat can be removed from the oven and served. But to cook your meat to perfection, you need to feel the meat. Give it a gentle prod with your finger: if the meat feels hard, it will be tough and chewy; however, if the meat feels soft and doesn't readily spring back, your meat will be lovely and soft once it has rested.

TROUBLESHOOTING

PROBLEM: **Even though the meat has reached 170°F (75°C), it is still tough.**

SOLUTION: **Don't worry too much because during the resting process the flesh will soften. However, if you find that the meat still has a lot of stringy toughness from connective tissue the only solution is to cook the meat longer to break down the collagen in the joint.**

PROBLEM: **You don't have time to slow roast a joint for a really long time.**

SOLUTION: **Revert to another cooking method. However, you can raise the** temperature of the cooking process to 210°F (100°C) to reduce the cooking time, although this will have a detrimental effect on the quality.

PROBLEM: **You want authentic pulled pork, smoke and all.**

SOLUTION: **Assuming you don't have a smoker, there are two handy tips that I can give you to imitate the effect. First, you can use already smoked meat such as a smoked picnic ham or leg ham. Second, when preparing your tray for roasting you can line it with tinfoil and cover it with smoking chips or sawdust in a layer approximately ¼-inch (6 mm) thick. Raise the cooking temperature to 210°F (100°C), and** place the tray of smoking chips above your meat. Use your oven's broiler to get the chips smoking, finally reverting to the oven only, with the door closed, for the remainder of the process. This turns your oven into a smoker. Unfortunately, this will stink up your kitchen (even if the oven door is kept closed and you have a really good exhaust fan), but it gets great results, so it is best done with all the doors and windows of your kitchen open.

Because this method has many of the same pitfalls as oven roasting, see the troubleshooting guide on page 41 for burned trivets, burned crackling, or crackling refusing to crackle.

Shoulder ready to carve

If you are making pulled pork, cook the meat until it falls apart with a gentle pull.

Unlike with oven roasting, there is no need to stop cooking the meat as soon as it has reached a safe temperature to eat because the quality of your roast will actually continue to improve with cooking as long as there is fat still present on the joint to keep the meat moist as it melts.

Serving the Pork

I. LET THE MEAT REST.

Take the meat to the warmest place in your kitchen, cover it with a clean tea towel, and let it rest for no less than 15 minutes for a small joint, 25 minutes for a large joint.

Unlike with oven roasting, the resting period can be much shorter here because the cooking temperature has been less aggressive, so you can get away with less resting time. However, if looking for perfection, the meat needs time to reach its optimum state, which is when the core temperature is 120°F (50°C), before you carve it.

2. CARVE THE MEAT.

If you are making pulled pork, place the meat in a large, deep pan and pull it apart with your hands. I use two latex disposable gloves on each hand to protect me from the heat and the meat from any pathogens. Alternatively, you can use two forks to pull the meat apart, but be careful not to shred the meat too finely, because it will dry out and become stringy.

Slow Roasting Experiments

In this section we'll explore two ways of taking your slow-roasted meat to the next level: using Cajun spices to pump up the flavor of pulled pork and making a smoked and glazed ham.

Cajun picnic roast spice-rubbed

Cajun pulled-pork rolls

Cajun-Spiced Pulled Picnic of Pork

This recipe will work with any slow-roasted pork joint and leave you with a sumptuous flavor-packed piece of meat that is so tender the only way to serve it is by pulling. The spice rub is easily substituted for any other dry rub, making this recipe fully customizable to obtain any flavored pulled pork you wish to make. You need to have your joint skinned to allow the rub to permeate the meat all over.

INGREDIENTS
Picnic of desired size
Cajun rub (page 145)

1. WASH, DRY, AND REFRIGERATE THE MEAT UNTIL READY TO USE.
See page 34.

2. APPLY CRACKLING RUB.
Using the Cajun rub, cover the entire piece of meat in a generous coating. Place your meat in the

Pulling pork

fridge for between 12 and 24 hours to allow the flavors to infuse the meat.

3. HOT FLASH THE MEAT.
Preheat the oven to 325°F (165°C, or gas mark 3). Place the meat in the oven for 10 to 15 minutes.

4. COOK THE MEAT.
After the initial hot flash, turn your oven down to 175°F (80°C) and continue cooking until the core temperature of the meat has reached 170°F (75°C), then continue cooking the meat for 30 to 45

HOT FLASHING WITH SPICE RUBS

Unlike the usual hot flash, we are going to only turn the oven up to 320°F (170°C, or gas mark 3) because if you turn the oven up much higher, the spices in the mix will scorch and you will end up with burned, acrid-tasting crust on your meat. This is the same reason why we skipped the sealing process.

Finished glazed ham

Removing the skin from cooked chilled ham

minutes longer, until the meat is tender enough to flake away from the bone.

5. LET THE MEAT REST.

Let the meat rest for a minimum of 15 minutes but ideally as long as it takes to cool to 120°F (50°C).

6. PULL THE MEAT APART.

Remove any bones from your meat; they will pull straight out of the meat because it is so tender. Then pull your meat apart using your fingers or two forks, dividing the more flavorful crust from the inner meat into separate bowls. Take your roasting pan and pour off the fat until you have roughly three-fourths meat juice and one-fourth fat. Add this to your pulled inner meat and toss the meat like you were dressing a salad.

7. SERVE THE MEAT.

Combine both bowls of meat, ensuring that the crust is equally distributed throughout, and serve.

Smoked and Glazed Ham

Okay, ham is not technically pork, but this is a great way to serve up a dinner and have fantastic sandwich filling for days after, and it can also take pride-of-place in a cold cuts feast.

INGREDIENTS

$^{1}/_{4}$ cup (45 g) whole cloves
1 cup (235 ml) pineapple juice
1 cup (225 g) firmly packed brown sugar
$^{1}/_{2}$ cup (170 g) honey
1 cup (235 ml) sweet sherry
1 cup (235 ml) chicken stock
Smoked ham of desired size

1. MAKE THE GLAZE.

Combine the cloves, pineapple juice, sugar, honey, sherry, and chicken stock in a large pan over high heat and cook until the consistency is that of cold maple syrup.

Glazing the ham

Carving a ham

2. COOK THE PLAIN HAM.

Cook the ham using the basic slow-roasting method without sealing or hot flashing the meat (see page 40) until the meat reaches 170°F (75°C). Allow the meat to cool and store it in the fridge overnight.

Remove the skin from the meat, leaving as much fat on the ham as possible. This will be easy because the fat will have cooked out and will be really soft and buttery; even the dullest knife will slide through it.

3. SCORE THE FAT.

Remove the ham from the fridge and place it on the trivets in a roasting pan. Score the fat in parallel lines every ³/₈ inch (1 cm), then score again in parallel lines at a not quite perpendicular angle to the first set of score marks, creating a diamond-shaped crosshatch pattern. Meanwhile, preheat the oven to 420°F (220°C, or gas mark 7).

4. APPLY THE GLAZE.

Warm the glaze over medium-low heat until the mix starts to soften. Use a pastry brush to paint a layer of the glaze all over the ham, ensuring that it gets a good coating.

5. CARAMELIZE THE GLAZE.

Place the ham into the oven for 5 minutes to allow the glaze to caramelize to the meat. Remove the ham from the pan and apply another layer of glaze, then return to the oven for 3 to 5 minutes longer. Continue to coat the ham and then caramelize the glaze for 3 to 5 minutes for six to ten cycles, until the glaze has become thick and shiny as the layers have built up.

6. SERVE THE MEAT.

Your glazed ham needs to sit on the trivets as it cools to allow the glaze to harden for roughly 20 to 30 minutes before refrigerating. When ready to serve, remove the meat from the fridge and slice as thinly as possible.

Signature Dish: Pork and Caramelized Apple Terrine

This recipe doesn't technically involve a roasting method per se, but what would any pork-specific book be without a little confit? Confit is the process of slow cooking meat in fat. It sounds disgusting until you have tried it. The fat cooking medium acts twofold as a moisturizer:

Plated terrine cold

It prevents a lot of the water in the meat from escaping, and the fat itself permeates the meat and adds extra moisture. This confit process and its resultant soft, moist meat lends itself to the traditional art of charcuterie making: terrines and rillettes made with the meat are soft, moist, and highly flavorful.

This recipe utilizes the traditional accompaniment of applesauce, which has been deconstructed and reworked into pockets of sweet caramelized apple that will explode contrasting flavors into your mouth as you work your way through the terrine.

For this recipe, each pound (455 g) of boneless shoulder or pork belly will make a generous lunch portion or a starter portion for two. This recipe should not be done with less than 5 pounds (2.3 kg) of meat, because if any smaller there would be too little meat to bind properly when pressing the terrine.

Confit setup

INGREDIENTS

At least 5 pounds (2.3 kg) boneless shoulder or pork belly

2 or 3 carrots, split in half

Duck fat or melted lard

Salt and pepper

3.5 ounces (90 g) firm, crisp-fleshed apples (such as Granny Smith) per 1 pound (455 g) of pork, unpeeled and cut into ¼-inch (6 mm) cubes

Lemon juice

Sugar

6 tablespoons (90 ml) water

Finely chopped parsley

Finely chopped shallot (roughly one-fourth the weight of the apples)

2. Cooked confit pork

For Pan Frying (Optional)

INGREDIENTS

Flour seasoned with salt and fine white pepper

2 or 3 eggs, beaten and mixed with 2 to 4 tablespoons (30 to 60 ml) milk

Bread crumbs

Oil or confit fat

1. CONFIT THE PORK.

Preheat the oven to 180°F (85°C). Place the meat in a roasting dish that fits as snugly to your meat as possible without it touching the sides of the dish. Place the carrots on the bottom of the pan to raise the pork, add either duck fat (preferable) or another meat fat to the tray until the meat is covered with the fat. Place the meat into the oven and cook until the core temperature has reached 175°F (80°C). Once the meat has reached this temperature, check it by pulling on a corner; if the meat pulls away easily, it's done. If not, check every 15 minutes until it is.

2. SHRED THE MEAT.

Allow the meat to rest and cool for at least an hour in the fat before removing it. Shred the meat into pieces (as with pulled pork; see page 65) into a large mixing bowl and season with salt and pepper to taste.

3. PREPARE THE APPLES.

Place the apples in a bowl and give them a generous squeeze of lemon juice to coat them and prevent them from browning.

4. Sugar carmelizing around the edges

4. Sugar carmelizing ¼ done

4. CARAMELIZE THE APPLES.

Heat a frying pan large enough to fit the apples comfortably over medium-high heat for 5 minutes. Use an equal weight of sugar to the amount of apples you're using and place the sugar in the pan, making sure it is spread evenly across the bottom. After 3 to 5 minutes the sugar around the perimeter of the pan will start to melt and brown. At this point shake the pan to redistribute the sugar.

Allow the caramelization to continue until about one-quarter of the sugar has liquefied and started to brown; at this point, start to stir the caramel gently with a wooden spoon.

Continue stirring until all the sugar has melted and browned, leaving you with a dark amber liquid that resembles runny honey. This should take roughly 10 to 12 minutes from start to finish.

4. Tossed apples

Cooling apples

MAKING CARAMEL ON A GAS STOVE

If using a gas stove, make sure that the flame is not so wide that it is licking up the sides of the pan because this will burn your caramel around the edges before the rest has caramelized.

Add the water to the caramel and allow it to dissolve the sugar.

Add the apples to the mix, being careful not to splash caramel on you because this would really hurt. Toss the apples through the caramel until it has completely melted again and coated your apples with a layer of caramel. Use a slotted spoon to remove the apples from the caramel and lay them out on some waxed paper.

5. The mixing bowl

Note: The leftover caramel makes a lovely dessert sauce: Heat to soften and add an equal measure of heavy cream.

5. BRING IT ALL TOGETHER.
Pour off the excess fat from the roasting pan until you are left with only the meat juices. Add enough of the juices to moisten the meat mixture in the bowl. Mix thoroughly. Add the parsley, caramelized apples, and shallots. Stir to combine thoroughly.

6. ASSEMBLE THE TERRINE.
Take some of the fat from the roasting tray and warm it a little so that it is completely liquid but not hot. Pour a little of the fat into the meat mixture and mix through. Keep on adding small increments of fat to the mix until you can feel the meat mix become noticeably moist and you hear a "squelch" if you give the mix a gentle squeeze.

On a table, create a double thickness of plastic wrap that is roughly 5 inches (12.7 cm) longer than your mold and 8 inches (20.3 cm) wider. Line the terrine mold with this double layer of plastic wrap and smooth it to the outside of the mold (lightly oiling the terrine will cause the plastic to stick to the metal). Pack the mixture into the terrine, trying to get as many of the meat strands to run in the lengthwise direction of the mold. Fold the side overhangs of wrap over the terrine and smooth on top, then do the same with the overhanging ends, ensuring that you have forced out any air bubbles that are under the wrap.

6. Filling terrine

Place something stiff that is the same size as the top of the terrine (another terrine mold is perfect but a piece of wood or metal that fits reasonably snugly will do) on top, weight it down with 2¹⁄₂ to 4¹⁄₂ pounds (1.1 to 2 kg), and place in the fridge for at least 24 hours before you remove the weights.

6. Pressing terrine

7. SERVE THE TERRINE.

The terrine is fantastic served cold or hot, depending on how you seasoned the meat.

If you intend to serve the terrine cold, you simply treat it as a pâté, slicing it to your required thickness and serving it up with some hot toast and a few cornichons to enjoy as a light lunch or starter.

Hot: Serving the terrine hot involves dipping slices of the meat into flour, egg wash, and bread crumbs (panne), then either deep- or shallow-frying to crisp the coating while the meat heats through.

7. Cold terrine ready to serve

SAVE THE FAT

Store the remaining fat in a container in the fridge and it will keep for a month; it can be used as confit fat for meats or to make killer roast potatoes.

Panne set up

1. Cut the terrine into slices no thicker than 1 inch (2.5 cm).

2. Set up three bowls, one filled with the seasoned flour, the next with the beaten eggs, and the last with the bread crumbs.

3. Take each slice and cover it in flour, patting the excess from the terrine gently. Dip it into the egg wash and remove, ensuring that the egg has coated the entire slice and allowing the excess to dribble off for a few seconds. Finally, dip it into the bread crumbs, ensuring that the whole thing gets a good covering of crumb.

4. Repeat the egg and bread crumb steps to make a double coating.

5. Place finished slices on a plastic wrap–lined tray, ensuring that they don't touch each other. These will keep in the fridge for about a day before the bread crumb layer starts to get too soggy to work properly.

6. To deep-fry, cook the slices in a deep-fat fryer set to 350°F (180°C), making sure that you don't overcrowd the fryer, and cook until the bread crumbs have taken on a lovely golden brown color all over. To shallow-fry, heat $\frac{1}{4}$ inch (6 mm) of the confit fat in a frying pan over medium-high heat; the fat is ready when a piece of bread turns golden brown in 60 seconds. Fry both sides of the terrine until golden.

7. Once cooked, lay the terrine slices on some kitchen towels to absorb the excess oil, and then you're ready to serve.

FOOD TEMPERATURE AND PROPER SEASONING

When seasoning food, it is essential to remember that if the food you are seasoning is going to be served hotter than the temperature at which you season it, you must under-season your food; if it is going to be served cooler, then you must over-season your dish. In this case, the food will be around room temperature, so if you are going to serve your meat cold, over-season and if you're serving it hot, under-season.

Deep-fried terrine finished

This terrine method is actually quite simple and very versitile, because once you have the confit you can pretty much choose what to add as the flavorings. Chopped apricots and pistachios is a great one. But you can add any dry flavorings you want as long as they are chopped to no larger than ½-inch (1.3 cm) pieces.

ADDING SPICES

If you are going to add dry spices to the mixture, remember you need to fry them first because the terrine will not be cooked. The best method is to fry the spices with some diced onion, then use a blender to turn the mixture into a spice paste so that you can add it to the meat mixture when seasoning to ensure that you have the correct balance.

CHAPTER 4

Pan Roasting ★★★★★

If I were to only teach you one cooking technique in this book, I would choose this one. It's in very few cookbooks, yet every culinary college will teach it (well, chefs have to keep something to set us apart). A roasting book without this totally indispensable method is verging on criminal, so I'm going to let you in on the secrets.

Pan roasting allows you to save time in the kitchen and deliver a thick cut of meat to the table perfectly cooked with an amazing, meaty, seared crust and juicy meat throughout. It also gives you much better results than pan frying because it promotes even cooking throughout the meat, especially with thicker cuts, making it a great everyday method as well as (with prior preparation) a great dinner party meal. The only downside of pan roasting is that you have to use the more expensive, tender cuts of meat in most cases to obtain the best results.

This time, we'll use the center-cut loin steak because it's probably the easiest to roast with great results. However, this method is great for all forms of thick-cut steaks and cuts of meat (more than 1 inch [2.5 cm] thick), not just pork.

Which Joints Are Best?

As with oven roasting, you are looking to the more tender cuts to get the best results with this technique, making any cut from the loin a great pan roaster.

Pan-roasted chops

TENDERLOIN STEAK

Ease of roasting ★★★★☆

Flavor ★★☆☆☆

Tenderness of end result ★★★★★

Quality of crackling N/A

Cost ★☆☆☆☆

Seared tenderloin steak

Everyone loves a good (beef) filet of steak, and pork tenderloin is the filet's counterpart in the pig. As such, it has the same characteristics (except smaller and cheaper) as the best tender cuts of beef. Like filet of beef is to a cow, the tenderloin is to a pig, having little connective tissue and a small amount of fat. These traits make pan-roasted tenderloin steak really tender, and if cooked correctly, a really juicy piece of meat that even the pickiest of meat eaters will finish every morsel of. The downside is that per pound tenderloin is the most expensive cut of meat on a pig.

PROS

- Almost no connective tissue, so really soft, tender meat
- Mild in flavor, so great for the recovering vegetarian
- Feeds one to twenty-five people
- Really moist, juicy flesh
- Really lean, so a good choice if you wish to reduce your fat intake

CONS

- Most expensive cut of pork
- Because it has very little fat, it is easy to overcook and dry out the meat
- Lacks rich meaty depth of flavor of other better-marbled cuts

Butcher's Notes

The filet of pork is the epitome of what you are looking for in a pan-roasting cut. It's naturally tender and has a fantastic texture that is really pleasurable to eat. This cut is quick to defrost, quick to cook, and easy to store due to its long, thin shape.

Pan roasting is the best way to get the most flavor from tenderloin, because the high heat of both the pan and the oven causes the fantastic browning Maillard reaction, giving a comparatively flavorless cut of meat a rich flavor that you will not get with other roasting methods. This really improves the tenderloin eating experience; by adding a deep, rich meat flavor as a foil to the excellent texture, you will see why the tenderloin is the most expensive cut of pork.

CENTER-CUT LOIN STEAK

Ease of roasting ★★★★☆

Flavor ★★★☆☆

Tenderness of end result ★★★★★

Quality of crackling N/A

Cost ★★☆☆☆

Seared loin steak

This cut is taken from the center section of the whole loin muscle, where it's the most tender and succulent. The cut itself is purely the eye of meat that runs the length of the loin, with a thin, solid layer of back fat around the top of the steak. As with the aforementioned tenderloin, the center-cut loin steak comes from the loin area of the pig and as such the flesh has similar qualities but is a modicum cheaper per pound and substantially larger. The layer of fat helps give the meat a little more flavor than that of the tenderloin and keeps the moisture in the meat during cooking.

PROS
- A cheaper alternative to tenderloin
- A more flavorful alternative to tenderloin
- Feeds one to twenty-five people
- Readily available

CONS
- Although cheaper than tenderloin, is still relatively expensive
- Has little fat marbling, so will dry out relatively quickly

Butcher's Notes

This is a great piece of meat and is preferable to the tenderloin due to its added flavor and reduced price tag. Of all the tender cuts of pork, this is the one that will have fussy eaters consuming everything while leaving those that prize flavor over ease of eating with a little of what they like as well. This cut is really tender and packs a lovely rich flavor (for a tender cut); it has a layer of fat on the outside and a different texture than the large, solid, and highly tender eye of the loin. To me, this is a really good alternative to the tenderloin, because it is cheaper, slightly easier to cook, and more flavorful while being almost as tender.

RIB CHOP

Ease of roasting ★★★★☆

Flavor ★★★★☆

Tenderness of end result ★★★★☆

Quality of crackling N/A

Cost ★★☆☆☆

The rib chop, like the previous cuts of meat, comes from the loin section of the animal. This cut comes from the front end of the loin just behind the shoulder and is analogous to the rib eye of beef. Unlike the other loin cuts of pork, though, this cut is widely available bone-in or boneless, giving you the choice. The rib chop comprises two different sections of meat: The lean solid eye muscle that contrasts nicely with the fattier, more flavorful section that is structured similarly to the belly (called the tail).

On top of the two areas of contrasting meat, there is a layer of back fat, which also helps add flavor and moisture to the meat as it cooks. Due to its close proximity to the shoulder, this area of the loin does work a little harder during the pig's lifetime, making the flesh marginally tougher than that of other loin cuts. However, this makes the meat more flavorful and creates a better marbling of fat—adding further flavor and helping to retain moisture when cooked.

PROS
- Feeds a variety of tastes, ranging from the fussy to die-hard flavor seekers
- Good balance of flavor and tenderness

Seared rib chop

- Feeds one to twenty
- Relatively hard to dry out (for a loin cut)
- Relatively cheap (for a loin cut)

CONS
- Not great for those looking for a lean cut of meat (although you can cut around the fat)
- Very difficult to get the eye and the tail to cook at the same rate

Butcher's Notes
This is a great everyday cut of pork to pan roast. It combines flavor, marbling, and a reasonable price tag with the added benefit of having contrasting textures and flavors to really keep your palate interested. The only downside is that, without playing around to render more fat from the tail, the intramuscular fat there tends to be stringy and not particularly pleasant to eat, so the meat within has to be worked for but is well worth it when it has been extracted.

CENTER-CUT HAM STEAK

Ease of roasting ★★★☆☆

Flavor ★★★★☆

Tenderness of end result ★★★☆☆

Quality of crackling N/A

Cost ★★☆☆☆

Seared center cut ham steak

The center-cut ham steak is exactly as the name describes: a steak cut through the ham (leg joint), leaving the bone in the center. A raw ham steak is something that is not particularly common in American markets, but it can be found at a butcher shop (or at least requested). Center-cut leg steak is widely available elsewhere in the world and is commonly referred to as gammon steak; it is mainly sold cured or smoked.

Because the steak is taken from the leg, the flesh itself tends to be slightly tough when cooked, if it is fresh. This is why it is best to get (if available) a cured or smoked steak because these processes have the effect of tenderizing the meat, making them both far superior to fresh ham steak when it comes to pan roasting. Beyond the slightly tough flesh, the rest of its characteristics make this a good, cheap, pan-roasting cut with plenty of fat to keep the cut moist and add great flavor from the outside while the bone radiates flavor into the meat from the middle, speeding the cooking time.

PROS
- Really cheap
- Great flavor
- Feeds one to ten people
- Also comes cured or smoked

CONS
- Can be a little tough
- Cured or smoked hams have a really high salt content.
- Can be hard to find in the United States

Butcher's Notes

Center-cut leg steaks are a thing of wonder that need to be shared. Fresh ham steaks are a little tough and benefit from a good marinade. Cured ones are good eating, but what gets this cut into this section is the smoked steak. The curing process helps to tenderize and moisten the meat; then the smoking adds an amazing complexity to the flavor of the pork, which comes alive when seared. They are also really cheap if you can find them and are an ideal way of eating tasty pork steaks for a low price.

Sealed loin steak going in oven

Preparing Pork for Pan Roasting

So, you've selected your cut of meat; now you can get ready to pan roast it. The preparations for the meat in the previous two chapters were remarkably similar because they were looking at preparing large joints of meat for dry oven cooking. With pan roasting, you are looking at more variations between the techniques, because this method is used primarily on small, tender cuts. However, a lot of the skills, equipment, and principles you use for oven roasting are the same. Once you have freed the meat from any packaging, you are ready to start preparing it.

1. WASH, DRY, AND REFRIGERATE THE MEAT UNTIL READY TO USE.
See page 34.

2. CUT THE FAT.
If your meat has no back fat or skin on it, skip to step 4.

Using a pair of scissors or a sharp knife, cut all the way through the skin and fat from one side of the

2. Scoring the fat

steak to the other. Repeat this every
$^1\!/_2$ inch (1.3 cm) or so all over the fat.

Cutting slits in the fat is important because it helps render the fat from the meat, make the fat palatable, and baste the meat. It also prevents the shrinking skin and fat that causes the meat to curl up.

3. AGE THE MEAT.
Place the meat on a cooling rack, uncovered, with plenty of space for air to move around each of the cuts, and leave in the fridge for 24 to 48 hours. Refrigerating it uncovered and unrubbed replicates the hanging process of meat, thus aging it.

This is a fantastic home-aging trick that a wizened old chef taught me, and it's a fantastic way to improve the quality of your meat. As the air circulates in the fridge, it will start to dry your meat, intensifying the flavor while also tenderizing it. I do the preparation up to this point with almost all small cuts of meat as soon as I get them home

3. Aging set up

from the market so they will be ready when I want to move on to the next step. It only adds another 15 minutes to the already boring chore of putting the shopping away, but it makes your meat even better. This can be done for longer than 48 hours with red meats such as beef, lamb, and venison, but should be limited to 48 hours for pork.

4. SEASON THE MEAT.

Once the meat has aged, season it with just table salt, ensuring that all the meat is seasoned.

At this stage the meat should have nothing on its surface except the salt you have just added. This is important because almost all spices, including pepper, will burn at the temperature at which we are going to seal the meat. This burned spice will become acrid tasting and smelling and will perfume the crust of the meat with its flavor.

Cooking the Meat

1. PREPARE THE ROASTING PAN.

As with the pan-roasting procedure, preheat the oven to 320°F (170°C, or gas mark 3), clearing all clutter from the oven to allow for free airflow. Preheat a thick roasting tray (preferably cast iron because it holds heat better) in the oven; this will be your roasting pan. You should also organize your oven, making sure that you have enough space for any accompaniments so the oven door has to spend as little time open as possible during the cooking of the meat. A steady oven temperature is especially important for pan roasting because a significant dip in the oven temperature can cause the pan to lose heat to the point where the juices from the meat will start to pool in the pan and stop the browning reaction, thus robbing you of the flavor that is eponymous of pan roasting.

2. SEAL THE MEAT.

Before you start to seal your meat, it is essential that you allow it to come to room temperature. This is done by simply removing the meat from the refrigerator about an hour before you intend to cook and leaving it covered on the counter. By allowing your meat to come to room temperature, you even out the cooking process by helping the meat in the center of your cut reach a safe temperature in less cooking time, resulting in less moisture being lost from the meat.

When sealing pork, especially small cuts, I really like to use lard because this is the natural fat of the pig and adds a little more flavor to your pork, but

2. Sealed rib chop

2. Using tongs to seal fat

canola oil or another neutral-flavored oil with a high smoke point will still do fine.

You are now ready to seal the meat. For this, you need a pan with enough oil in it to cover the bottom by about the thickness of a knife's blade. Unlike sealing a whole joint, this oil needs to be lightly smoking hot to seal the meat.

Place the meat in the pan, ensuring, if you are cooking more than one, that they are not overcrowded. Fry the meat until a light browning has occurred (if the pan is hot enough this should happen in about 45 to 60 seconds). Repeat this for all the surfaces of the meat. If the cut of meat has a layer of fat around it, you need to ensure that this has really started to crisp during the sealing process because it will have little time to crisp up in the oven.

3. INSERT THE PROBE AND PLACE THE PAN IN THE OVEN.

Remove your preheated roasting pan from the oven and place it over medium heat on the stove top (to help the pan hold its heat out of the oven). Arrange the meat, giving it as much space in the tray as possible, and replace the pan in the oven. Add the fat from the pan so that this can continue

USE CAUTION

Now I know that a lot of you are going to look at your pan and worry that you are going to burn your house down. You're not. As long as you have only a barely visible haze of smoke, not clouds billowing from the pan, there is no way lard or any other high-smoke-point oil will catch fire. Never take your eyes off the pan while it heats up, though, because this can happen more quickly than you might expect.

CHEF'S TIP

You can actually roast your meat up to a day after sealing it if the meat is refrigerated straight after sealing. This is especially useful if you are cooking for a party because you will have done all the hard work the day before, leaving you to just cook the meat and worry about the accompaniments on the day of the gathering. You just need to ensure that your meat is at room temperature before you move on to the roasting.

to aid in the roasting and basting process. If you have an in-oven temperature probe, place it in a steak at the center of the pan, entering the steak from the side.

It is key to pan-roasting that your pan should stay hot enough to continue the browning reaction throughout the cooking process. Whenever you have to remove the pan from the oven, remember to set it over medium heat to keep that heat in the pan.

4. COOK THE MEAT.

Once your meat is in the oven, leave it alone for the first 5 minutes, then, hopefully as quick as a ninja, you can open your oven, flip all the meat, and close the door in less than 30 seconds. If you can't because of the sheer number of portions being cooked, remove the pan, place it over medium heat (you know the drill), and flip them out of the oven. Repeat this, probably twice. A $1\frac{1}{2}$-inch (3.8 cm) thickness of pork takes about 14 minutes, but it depends on the cut, so always ensure the meat has reached 145°F (63°C).

4. Rib chops in pan

By flipping the meat as it roasts in the oven, you ensure that both sides get seared evenly on the bottom of the pan, getting great color while not overcooking or drying out one side of the meat.

5. REMOVE THE PORK FROM THE OVEN.

Remove the pork from the oven as soon as the core temperature reaches 145°F (63°C). By removing the meat when it has reached its safe temperature of 145°F (63°C), you have ensured that the core has reached the safe temperature to eat while not causing the proteins in the meat to shrink and squeeze out moisture. While the meat rests, the residual heat finishes it off to a core temperature of 150° to 155°F (65° to 68°C), meaning that it is ever so slightly pink in the middle and not overcooked (but safe to eat), while keeping the meat juicy and moist.

Serving the Meat

As with the previous two cooking methods, the resting time is all-important to the final quality of the meat. However, because these cuts of meat are so much smaller, a higher percentage of the water in the cut will escape, making the meat dry and robbing it of flavor. Resting your meat is possibly the most important stage in pan roasting to ensure it remains moist after cooking.

1. Resting the meat

TROUBLESHOOTING

PROBLEM: The meat stops sizzling.

SOLUTION: This means the temperature of your pan has dropped too much. This is a clear indicator that one of two things has occurred. First, and most likely, your pan is not up to pan roasting because it can't hold its heat during the cooking process. As stated above, it is essential to use a thick roasting pan or frying pan that will hold its heat. Simply buy a different roasting pan if you wish to pan roast. To get you through this roast, crank the heat up to 180°C (85°C), pull the pan out of the oven, put it on the stove top, and get it sizzling again over high heat, turning the meat before replacing the tray in the oven to finish off.

Second, you may have overcrowded the pan, meaning the roasting tray cannot retain its heat. This is simply avoided by not overcrowding the pan in the first place. The only way to save this is to act fast and heat another pan through quickly over high heat so that you can decant the meat into the other larger pan to finish off the cooking.

PROBLEM: The meat is starting to stick on the bottom of the pan.

SOLUTION: This will only occur close to the end of the cooking process, so the easiest way to stop the meat from burning is to deglaze the pan with the meat still in it and return to the oven to finish. Okay, I said the pan needs to be sizzling all the way through the cooking process, but that's to ensure that the meat is browned enough. If it has started to burn, it has already browned fully, so stopping the Maillard reaction is not an issue because it is en route to being over-browned or burned. Once deglazed, remove any liquid from the pan and save for gravy if it has not taken on a burned flavor, and return your meat to the oven.

1. LET THE MEAT REST.

Place your meat in a warm spot in your kitchen and let it rest for a minimum of 5 minutes, but preferably for 10 minutes for $1\frac{1}{2}$ inches (3.8 cm) of thickness of your steak.

As stated before, resting the meat helps it retain its moisture and is essential to great meat quality.

2. SERVE THE MEAT.

Simply serve your meat either with its accompaniments as complete meals or on a warmed plate for people to serve themselves family-style and relax and enjoy.

This is the great thing about pan roasting: it allows you to get most of your preparation done before you actually start cooking, with only the actual roasting and resting having to occur anywhere near service time. This leaves you plenty of time to enjoy your own party, because the majority of work can be done beforehand.

THE SCIENCE OF RESTING

As the meat starts to cook, the proteins and the collagen start to contract, squeezing the water molecules from the cells in the meat. When you remove your steak from the heat, the meat continues to cook due to the heat still inside, thus continuing to squeeze the water from the cells. As you can see when you squash the meat, a large amount of liquid is pushed from it. This juice would have made your steak juicy and lovely if rested.

Everyone has been confronted by pools of blood at the bottom of your plate, making your fries and onion rings soggy. This is meat that hasn't been rested, pure and simple, so I implore you to rest your meat. After this, if you do eat an unrested piece of meat without a good reason, I would honestly say you are beyond help.

Pan Roasting Experiments

In this section we'll explore two ways of taking your pan-roasted pork to the next level, by flavoring it with sage and with Jamaican jerk seasoning.

Pan-Roasted Sage-Scented Tenderloin of Pork

INGREDIENTS

Tenderloin of pork of desired size
Basic marinade (page 146)
Large sage leaves, finely chopped
Several cloves garlic, split in half

1. WASH, DRY, AND REFRIGERATE THE MEAT UNTIL READY TO USE.

See page 34.

2. MARINATE THE MEAT.

Mix enough of the basic marinade recipe to totally cover all the cuts of meat you intend to serve. Add about three finely chopped large sage leaves per portion to the marinade. Place all your meat into a food bag and pour the marinade over it. Place in the fridge and allow to stand for 24 hours. Remove the meat from the marinade and pat dry with paper towels.

3. SEAL THE MEAT.

See page 82.

4. COOK THE MEAT.

Take your sealed meat and place it into the roasting pan with the sealing fat. To this add one sage leaf and ½ clove of garlic (spilt lengthways) for every portion. Make sure these are spread evenly throughout the pan and roast as per page 83.

2. Marinating meat in a bag

The sage and garlic will flavor the cooking oil, which will add extra flavor to the crust of the meat. This is a great way of adding extra flavor to the meat and any herbs and spices (such as rosemary, thyme, or fresh peppercorns) will work because there is not enough time in the roasting process to burn them.

5. LET THE MEAT REST.

Allow your meat to rest for a minimum of 8 minutes per 1 inch (2.5 cm) of thickness of meat, but ideally until the core temperature has fallen to 120°F (50°C).

6. SERVE.

Transfer the meat onto warmed plates and use some of the crisped sage leaves as a garnish.

3. Marinate the meat

Jamaican Jerk Pork Chops

INGREDIENTS

Pork chops of desired size

Basic marinade (page 146)

1. WASH, DRY, AND REFRIGERATE THE MEAT UNTIL READY TO USE.

See page 34.

2. CUT THE FAT.

See page 66.

3. MARINATE THE MEAT.

Make up enough of the jerk marinade to cover all of the meat you wish to serve. Place your meat in a freezer bag and pour your marinade into the bag, reserving about ½ tablespoon (8 ml) of marinade per portion to act as a finishing drizzle. Allow the meat to marinate for up to 24 hours before removing it from the marinade and patting it dry with paper towels.

7. Finished pork chop

4. SEAL THE MEAT.

See page 81.

5. COOK THE MEAT.

See page 83.

6. LET THE MEAT REST.

See page 85.

7. SERVE THE MEAT.

Serve your meat on a warmed plate and finish the meat off with a little drizzle of the reserved marinade.

Finished escalope

Signature Dish: Herb-Crusted Pork Escalope

Stuffed with Vine-Ripened Tomato and Mozzarella

This is actually a rather simple dish that requires a degree of hard work, but it will pay off in the long run because you will have a treat for dinner and be able to wow any guests into thinking you spent at least a few years working in professional kitchens. This recipe is also highly therapeutic because you will see how to create your own escalope with a rolling pin, some baking parchment, a little oil, and some controlled violence. For this, we will be using the eye of the loin steak with the fat removed and cut to a 1 to 1^{1}/$_{2}$-inch (2.5 to 3.8 cm) thickness. You can buy escalope, but it is easier to stuff it using the method below. The stuffing can be replaced by anything you like: garlic, herb butter, ham and Gruyère, or even some apple and cranberry compote for a festive meal. You can get really creative with this. Have fun.

INGREDIENTS

Center-cut pork steaks of desired size

Buffalo mozzarella, thinly sliced

Fresh, vine-ripened tomato, thinly sliced

Basil leaves, stems removed

Salt and finely ground black pepper

Flour seasoned with salt and fine white pepper

2 or 3 eggs, beaten and mixed with 2 to 4 tablespoons (30 to 60 ml) milk

Bread crumbs mixed with dry Italian herb mix (add 1 teaspoon dry Italian herb mix for every 1 cup [115 g] bread crumbs)

Oil, for frying

1. WASH, DRY, AND REFRIGERATE THE MEAT UNTIL READY TO USE.

See page 34.

2. Cut your escalope

3. Pounding out escalope

2. CREATE THE ESCALOPE.

Using a sharp, long-bladed knife, cut through the center of the steak until you have about $^{1}/_{2}$ inch (1.3 cm) left before you have cut your steak completely in half. Open out your steak so that it makes a shape that resembles a butterfly.

3. POUND OUT THE ESCALOPE.

Place your meat onto a lightly oiled piece of waxed paper and place another sheet on the top, covering

with a dish towel. Pound the meat with a heavy rolling pin. This requires the application of some force, but not excessive. Continue to pound the meat until it is about ¼-inch (6 mm) thick all over.

4. STUFF THE ESCALOPE.

Lay a couple of slices of buffalo mozzarella in the center of one of the wings of the butterfly. Add a couple of slices of fresh ripe tomato and two basil leaves. Season the side of the meat that is facing

3. Batted out escalope

4. Stuffing the escalope

4. Floured escalope

4. Egged escalope

you with salt and finely ground black pepper. Fold over the meat so that it meets the other wing of the butterfly. Make sure the filling is in the center of the pocket and not near the edges. Press the edges of the meat together firmly and refrigerate for 30 minutes.

4. SEAL THE ESCALOPE.

Set up three bowls, one filled with the seasoned flour, the next with the beaten eggs, and the last with the bread crumbs. Take each slice and cover it in flour, patting the excess from the escalope gently. Dip it into the egg wash and remove, ensuring that the egg has coated the entire slice and allowing the excess to dribble off for a few seconds. Finally, dip it into the bread crumbs, ensuring that the whole thing gets a good covering of crumb. Repeat the egg and bread crumb steps to make a double coating.

Place finished slices on a plastic wrap–lined tray, ensuring that they don't touch each other. These will keep in the fridge for about a day before the bread crumb layer starts to get too soggy to work properly. When ready to cook, remove from the fridge and allow to come to room temperature.

4. Breaded escalope

5. FRY THE ESCALOPE.

Preheat a frying pan, with roughly ½ inch (1.3 cm) oil in the bottom, over medium heat so that when a piece of bread is placed in the pan it takes roughly a minute to brown. Place the escalope into the pan and fry for about 1 minute, until the escalope has lightly browned, then remove from the pan.

6. COOK THE ESCALOPE.

Preheat the oven to 350°F (180°C, or gas mark 4). Place the escalope on a dry roasting tray (the bread crumb coating will have absorbed enough fat) and roast for 8 to 12 minutes, until the meat has reached 145°F (63°C) on a meat thermometer. Be careful not to stick the thermometer into the center of the pocket, because this will be cheese and tomato and will not give you an accurate reading.

7. LET THE ESCALOPE REST.

Allow the meat to rest for 5 to 10 minutes.

8. SERVE.

Transfer the meat onto warmed plates and enjoy.

Next comes the sauce lover's heaven of pot roasting. Think melting meat and sticky sauces— not to mention that intoxicating aroma drifting from the kitchen to tempt you to the table. It's the last of our home-roasting techniques, with a few cheeky twists thrown in for good measure.

5. Frying the escalope

6. Browned escalope on baking sheet

CHAPTER 5

Pot Roasting ★★★★★

Pot roasting is the simplest method to play with the flavors you add to your meat. You cook the pork in its own sauce or gravy, meaning that you can impart any flavor you wish by adding it to the sauce without using a spice rub or marinade. This is the easiest way to make a fantastic rich and intense sauce while providing you with really gorgeous, flavorful meat.

This is a great technique for cheaper, tougher cuts of pork because the fat and connective tissue that hold the meat together are slowly broken down (converting insoluble collagen into soluble gelatin) during the cooking process. This leaves the meat "melt-in-the-mouth soft," because much of the connective tissue breaks down and is released into the sauce as gelatinous juices, leaving the meat tender but helps make rich, thick, full-bodied gravy.

Pot roasting is a great method to learn because not only does it give you another delicious way of cooking meat but it is also a fantastic way of learning about sauces that go beyond simple pan juice gravies.

Which Joints Are Best?

When deciding on a joint to pot roast, it is best to choose a tough cut that is well covered with fat. Cuts like this have the most flavor but also contain the most collagen, which breaks down and then emulsifies into your sauce and helps thicken it. It is possible to pot-roast tender cuts if you wish, but there is not enough collagen to make a stunning sauce or to keep your meat super moist.

Finished pot roast shoulder

BELLY

Ease of roasting ★★★★★

Flavor ★★★★☆

Tenderness of end result ★★★★☆

Quality of crackling N/A

Cost ★★★★☆

Pot roasted belly

Pork bellies are wonderful pot roasters in an unconventional way. Pork belly itself has little collagen but instead has a marvelous fat structure that helps keep it moist during cooking. In pot roasting, a lot of this fat melts from the meat and enriches the sauce, giving it a more meaty taste than when using a higher-collagen, lower-fat cut. The downside of this is that you don't get a lot of the natural thickening of the gelatin in your sauce, meaning you will not have that wonderful palate-coating quality with a belly roast unless you add a roasted trotter to your cooking liquor.

Decide how you wish to serve the pork belly before buying it, because it has a long, flat shape. If you wish to serve it sliced like a traditional joint, you should purchase a rolled and tied joint. If you wish to serve your meat in portion-size slabs, buy a flat belly.

PROS
- Large amount of fat gives a rich flavor to your sauce
- Layers of fat keep the meat really moist and succulent
- Feeds four to twenty-four people

CONS
- This is a fatty cut, so you will end up with a large layer of grease on your gravy that will need to be removed
- Is relatively low in collagen so you will need to thicken your gravy more

Butcher's Notes

Belly is a particularly nice joint to pot roast due to its high and perfectly positioned fat content. Because the fat and meat are arranged in layers throughout the joint, the meat is surrounded by melting fat while cooking, which seals in the natural moisture. The fat that remains in the meat at the end of cooking then adds to the moistness of the meat when it comes to eating it. The only downside of this cut is that it has comparatively little connective tissue, so it doesn't add gelatin to the sauce and thus lacks the luxurious quality that other tougher cuts bring to their sauces.

BONED AND ROLLED SHOULDER

Ease of roasting ★★★★☆

Flavor ★★★★★

Tenderness of end result ★★★★★

Quality of crackling N/A

Cost ★★★☆☆

Boned and rolled shoulder

Boned and rolled shoulder cuts are smaller cuts taken from the Boston butt and, as such, share their qualities (which can be found in chapter 3). Boned and rolled shoulders are more suitable to home pot roasting because their smaller size allows more even cooking and tenderization. Obviously, the whole Boston butt itself is still great for pot roasting if you have a large enough pot.

PROS
- Good rich, meaty flavor
- Fat marbling provides great moisture
- Feeds four to twenty-eight people (for numbers larger than twelve it is preferable to roast two joints)
- Rolled joints cook more evenly

CONS
- Rolled joints can contain large deposits of fat in some places
- Large joints have a tendency to fall apart when carved

Butcher's Notes
Like the picnic, the shoulder has a really high level of collagen, giving the sauce from a pot roast a fantastic sticky quality. It also packs a great meaty flavor that will really shine through in your sauce. The main problem with the whole shoulder is its spherical shape, meaning that it is very hard to find a pot that it will fit into for roasting, although a smaller cut taken from the shoulder cooked in a large home casserole dish should be able to feed up to twelve.

LOIN OF PORK

Ease of roasting ★★★★☆

Flavor ★★★☆☆

Tenderness of end result ★★★★☆

Quality of crackling N/A

Cost ★★☆☆☆

Roasted loin

As you know from previous sections, the loin of pork is a tender cut, and it has a large layer of back fat that helps keep the meat moist during cooking. The innate tenderness of the cut means that the cooking time of the meat is greatly reduced because you don't have to wait for the tenderization to take place. The core temperature only needs to reach 145°F (60°C) to be ready to serve.

PROS

- Cooks more quickly because you don't have to tenderize the meat
- Great for picky eaters
- Feeds four to twenty-five people
- Carves very easily for a pot roast

CONS

- Very expensive cut to pot roast
- Very easy to overcook and end up with dry, stringy meat if you don't remove at 140°F (60°C)

Butcher's Notes

The loin of pork is not an amazing cut of pork to pot roast. However, it is the best of all the tender cuts and still gets pretty good results. This is because the meat is already tender and does not need to be cooked for a long time for the connective tissues to break down. As soon as your meat has reached a safe temperature, it is time to stop cooking. This has the downside that the meat has little time to impart flavor into the gravy and there is little collagen to render into the sauce to give it its natural palate-coating thickness.

CHEEKS

Ease of roasting ★★★★☆

Flavor ★★★☆☆

Tenderness of end result ★★★★☆

Quality of crackling

Cost ★★★★★

Pot roasted cheeks

The cheeks of the pig work really hard in the pig's lifetime; pigs eat a lot. Because this is a hard-working muscle, it contains a large amount of collagen, making the texture of the meat tough and fibrous if the meat is not tenderized before consumption. The constant work and the close proximity to the large jowl fat deposit means that the flesh can come with a covering of fat that helps keep it moist during cooking.

Five average-size pork cheeks will give you a large single portion, but a large one served with plenty of accompaniments can be stretched to feed two. This means that the limit to the number you can cook is however many you can fit into your pot-roasting pot. For the average home pan, this is about fifteen cheeks, but if you have a large pan you can fit more in.

PROS

- Possibly the cheapest chunk of meat you can get from the pig
- Solid chunk of meat on which, if tenderized, every morsel is edible
- Feeds one to fifteen people
- Gives your gravy a great palate-coating quality that makes the flavor of the juice linger in your mouth

CONS

- Can't be served as a joint
- People may be put off by the word *cheek*.

Butcher's Notes

The cheek is the hidden gem of the pig when it comes to pot roasting. It's absolutely useless for all other means of roasting, but pot-roasted pork cheek is absolutely divine; the best by quite a long way, not only for the quality of the meat but also for the amazing quality it brings to your gravy.

Cheeks have a very high collagen content that, when heated, turns into water-soluble gelatin that dissolves into the sauce, helping to thicken it while giving it a slightly sticky quality. This means as you eat a nice mouthful of pork and gravy, the gravy lingers on your palate a little longer, helping to really lift the flavor of your pork to new heights as the flavors develop in your mouth.

To look at, cheeks resemble the most perfectly tender piece of meat you would ever wish to cook, and although it has an ugly name, it is a really attractive piece of meat. Because this is not a widely used piece of meat, you may have some difficulty obtaining cheeks. However, if you have a local butcher who cuts down his own carcasses, he should be more than happy to prepare or call in as many of these underutilized delights for you as you wish.

Preparing Pork for Pot Roasting

INGREDIENTS

Per 1 pound (455 g) of meat, you will need:

1 small onion, finely diced or grated

½ stick celery, sliced

Salt

½ teaspoon milk powder

½ tablespoon (10 g) tomato purée

Chicken stock

Pre-roasted and browned chicken or pork bones

1. WASH, DRY, AND REFRIGERATE THE MEAT UNTIL READY TO USE

See page 34.

2. SEAL THE MEAT.

Get yourself an appropriately sized casserole or pot-roasting pot, and place it over high heat. Oil the pan lightly, and wait for the oil to start to smoke gently, then seal the meat to get a nicely browned crust all over. Because the rest of the cooking process will be in liquid, which can only reach a temperature of about 212°F (100°C), no more of the browning Maillard reaction will take place, so you need to get the meat as brown as you wish to serve it in the sealing stage. Remove it from the pan, transfer it to a plate, and move on to the next step.

2. Sealed shoulder for pot roast

3. PREPARE THE BASIC LIQUID.

Lower the heat under the pan to medium. Add the onions and celery that you have prepared, and start to fry them in the fat left in the pan from sealing the meat, adding a pinch of salt to help the process.

After 1 minute or so, add ½ teaspoon of milk powder per pound of meat to the mix (stir your pan regularly to prevent the mix from burning).

3. Sautéing ingredients in the pan

Deglazing the pan

Meat in pan with cooking liquor

After about another minute or two, when the onions are starting to brown, add ¹/₂ tablespoon (10 g) of tomato purée per pound of meat and mix it through the sautéing vegetables.

Add enough chicken stock so that when the meat is reintroduced, the level of the liquid will cover two-thirds of the meat.

Add any bones that you have from your meat (pre-roasted and browned) to the liquid. Adding a roasted pig's trotter to the mix will give your sauce a luxurious, palate-coating quality.

Heat the liquid until it just starts to simmer (this is roughly 180°F [85°C]).

Cooking the Meat

The above preparation of the sauce can be done up to three days prior to cooking. This is highly advisable if cooking a pot roast for a party and will be a huge weight off your mind come the day of

your event. If you wish to do this before you start cooking, you need to allow your meat to come to room temperature and heat the cooking liquid to 180°F (85°C) and the oven to 250°F (120°C, or gas mark ¹/₂) before you proceed. You should count on 45 minutes per pound (455 g) for tough cuts and 20 minutes per pound (455 g) for tender cuts.

1. PLACE THE MEAT IN THE ROASTING POT.
Preheat the oven to 250°F (120°C, or gas mark ¹/₂). Put the meat in with the liquid and cover with a lid, ensuring that your meat is not touching the sides or top of the pan, and insert your cooking thermometer. Place bones (if not available, a couple of carrots cut lengthwise will work as an adequate replacement) under the meat to lift it from the bottom of the pan and stop it from rolling into the sides and touching the metal during the cooking process. This is essential because the metal of your cooking pot will be much hotter than the liquid and will cause the

THE POT-ROASTING LIQUID

The reason you create the liquid in the above order is as follows:

1. Tossing in the onion and celery first allows them time to add color to the pan. This time it's not just the Maillard reaction but also the sugar caramelizing that causes the browning. The caramelized sugar notes of the onions will add a lovely depth of flavor to your sauce rather than giving it a noticeable sweetness. The aromatic quality of the celery works as a flavor enhancer for meat and adds an undernote of freshness to your sauce. The onions and celery (if chopped finely enough) will liquefy during cooking and help thicken the sauce, but will not be noticeable in the finished sauce.

2. Milk powder sounds like a really odd addition to a meat sauce, but milk is composed of the same key ingredients that are required for the Maillard reaction to occur. This means that as the milk powder browns, the Maillard reaction occurs and gives you additional roast meat flavor.

3. Adding tomato purée early and roasting quickly changes the taste from sweet and sour with a bitter aftertaste into a deep, rich tomato flavor which neutralizes that aftertaste. This is why all tomato paste should be roasted before adding it to any food. (This tip makes a huge difference in all dishes you cook, but I digress.) The deep, rich flavor of tomato adds another layer of flavor to your sauce. But the best thing about roasted tomato paste is that it contains compounds that actually massively boost meaty flavors while also helping to thicken the sauce.

4. Adding chicken stock to the pan is pretty basic; you need a liquid to pot roast in, so why just add bland water? Adding chicken stock (preferably homemade, but store-bought will do) provides a good meaty base to the sauce without deterring from the natural pork taste as beef or lamb stock would.

5. Adding roasted chicken or pork bones is a fantastic and cheap way to pack natural meaty flavors into your sauce. If you buy meat from a proper butcher, bones are a waste product of their trade and they will most likely give you a few for free if you ask them nicely. The effect of including bones in your sauce to add meaty flavors is obvious, but it is the addition of trotters that is really interesting—but I'll get there. The bones should be placed under your meat to prevent it from touching the metal of your pan and cooking unevenly.

You're probably bored of hearing this, so in short, trotters are high in collagen, collagen denatures when heated into gelatin, and gelatin is water-soluble. Gelatin thickens the sauce naturally, giving it that palate-coating quality. You don't need many to add many trotters; one will have the desired effect unless you are cooking for more than twelve people.

This allows you to imitate the mouth-lingering quality of sauces that have taken hours, sometimes days, to concoct in professional kitchens in the time it takes you to make a pot roast.

6. By heating the liquid to 180°F (85°C) or a low simmering point, you speed the process and get the cooking liquid to the perfect temperature for pot roasting.

2. Pot roast in the oven

meat to cook unevenly. The same applies to the lid: if it is placed on the pan and it touches the meat, don't use it. Instead, place a layer of parchment paper over the meat and seal the top of the pot with tinfoil (this won't hold as much heat as the lid but it will prevent the meat from cooking as unevenly), ensuring that the tinfoil lid will prevent the steam escaping.

2. COOK THE MEAT.

Once your roast is in the oven, all you need to do is turn your pork over every 30 minutes or so. This will ensure that both sides cook evenly and stay moist as each side will spend equal amounts of time in the cooking liquid.

If you intend to cook your accompanying vegetables with the pot roast, add them to the pan, allowing them 50 percent extra cooking time compared to if you had boiled them on the stove (e.g., small new potatoes that would take 15 minutes depending on size would require

an extra 7½ minutes). This will prevent all the natural goodness from being cooked out of them and destroyed. It is a common myth that all the goodness of vegetables would just transfer to your sauce. This is the case with many of the essential vitamins and minerals in vegetables, but a lot of them will be destroyed by the heat of the cooking process and lost forever. If you overcook the vegetables, you will also find that your meals become "mono-flavored," with your meat, sauce, and vegetable flavors melding into one flavor.

At the beginning of the section, I stated that a pot roast will take 45 minutes per pound (455 g) of meat (20 minutes for tender). This is a rough guide and should not be used as an accurate measure for how long your pork should be in the oven. There are so many factors that can change the cooking time; so many, in fact, that I'm not going to cover them—you are just going to have to trust me.

To cook tender cuts of meat such as loin of pork to perfection, simply remove your meat when the core temperature reaches 145°F (63°C), just as with oven roasting. Judge tougher cuts of meat in the same way as with slow roasting; the meat will be safe to eat when it has reached 150°F (65°C), but it will still be really tough because most of the connective tissue will not have been broken down. This means that you have to make the decision of how long you want to cook your meat based on how tender you want it to be before you remove it from the oven.

3. REMOVE THE PORK FROM THE OVEN.

When your meat is cooked, remove the roast from the oven.

Serving the Pork

I. LET THE MEAT REST.

Place your meat on a carving dish and allow the meat to rest until the core temperature has reached 120°F (50°C), or as long as possible, to allow the meat tissue to relax.

2. TURN THE LIQUID INTO SAUCE.

While your meat is resting, strain your cooking liquid into a saucepan. Allow the liquid to settle for a moment or two and remove any surface fat from the top. Place the pan over high heat and bring it to a boil, then taste. If the sauce is insipid and lacks flavor, simply keep it over the heat until it has reduced enough to heighten the flavor to your desired strength. If your sauce has all the punch you wish, there is no need to reduce your sauce, but it will most likely need a little

thickening. This can be done in a variety of ways, including gravy granules (if you want to ruin all your hard work), but I prefer whisking in a little bit of beurre manié (French for "kneaded butter") to finish most sauces.

3. CARVE THE MEAT.

There are two ways to approach carving pot roast, depending on whether the meat is boneless or bone-in.

Carving boneless meat is simple. Place your joint on a carving dish. Figure out which way the grain of the meat runs, and carve your meat into thick slices, making sure that you cut across the grain.

If the roast you are carving is bone-in, it's a little more like a surgical procedure because you need to remove each lump of meat and carve them individually. Start by holding the meat in place with your carving fork and figure out which piece you will remove from the joint first. Then use

1. Meat resting

3. Carving the pot roast

BEURRE MANIÉ

This is a great way to lightly thicken soups or sauces at the end of the cooking process and can be used to finish any sauce that needs it. Beurre manié consists of equal parts softened butter and flour mixed together to form a paste, with each of the flour particles coated in butter. When the beurre manié is whisked into a hot or warm liquid, the butter melts, releasing the flour particles without creating lumps.

Because beurre manié contains uncooked flour, it may leave an undesirable floury or pasty taste. For this reason, it is important that the beurre manié be allowed to cook adequately. Rather than being added to a dish immediately before serving, you should always give it at least 5 minutes of simmering time to allow the gluten to cook out. Beurre manié is also used as a finishing step for sauces, as it imparts a smooth, shiny texture, while the butter adds a smooth, rich flavor to the finish of the sauce.

Beurre manié

The amount of beurre manié needed to thicken your sauce is very much dependent on both the viscosity of your sauce prior to thickening and the desired consistency of your finished sauce. This is the main reason I prefer this method of finishing sauces to using a roux. Here are some rough guidelines:

3 ounces (84 g) of beurre manié per 1 quart (946 ml) of liquid = thin or light consistency

4 ounces (112 g) of beurre manié per 1 quart (946 ml) of liquid = medium-bodied sauce

5 ounces (140 g) of beurre manié per 1 quart (946 ml) of liquid = thick sauce

6 ounces (170 g) of beurre manié per 1 quart (946 ml) of liquid = heavy gravy

When adding beurre manié, always whisk in three-fourths of the amount in this guideline, because it is easy to add more beurre manié but impossible to remove, and simmer until the taste of raw flour is gone (10 to 20 minutes). Then, if it is required, add more and simmer again until the raw flavor is cooked out.

The one problem with beurre manié is that it will add white to the color of the sauce, so red sauces will turn pink and dark sauces will become lighter and will look weird in some cases. In these circumstances, I would revert to good old cornstarch or arrowroot.

the tip of your knife to cut between muscles, and follow the line of bones where possible to remove a solid piece of meat. Treat bones, muscles, and layers of fat as natural seams to the meat that are easy to follow. Once you have removed your first piece of meat, treat it like a small boneless joint and carve it into slices, cutting across the grain. Repeat this until every chunk of meat has been stripped from the bone and carved.

Pot Roasting Experiments

Rather than giving you two variations on the basic method, pot roasting is open to myriad changes while making the cooking liquid. This basic sauce is a fantastic sauce by itself, because it layers subtle flavors that all work well together, intensify and complement meaty flavors, and improve the texture and appearance of the sauce. It's also a great place to start experimenting with flavors, because it is the perfect base for many meat sauces.

You just have to understand which way to tailor the flavor at each stage.

In with the onions

At this point you can add:

ADDITIONAL AROMATIC VEGETABLES
These should be finely diced or sliced so they break down into the sauce. Onion, celery, and carrot form what in French cooking is called the mirepoix (*meer-pwah*), with leeks, fennel, and garlic being common staple additions. All add a little extra flavor while building up the layers of complexity in the sauce without changing the overall taste dramatically; they act as a great foundation on which to build.

If you wish to add any aromatics to your sauce, substitute them for some of the mirepoix mix, ensuring that your base is still mainly onion.

FRUIT
Fruit should be diced to the same size as the onion and celery to allow it to break down during the

Aromatic vegetables

Fruit

cooking process. Adding the fruit at this stage allows the sugars in the fruit to caramelize with those of the aromatic vegetables (having the same effect), allowing their flavor to come through in the sauce as well as the meat. If you wish to have chunks of fruit in your sauce these need to be added when finishing the sauce, because all fruit added at this stage will effectively liquefy during cooking.

Spices

Pork works best with fruit with a hint of an acidic bite, such as apricots, pineapple, pear, the ubiquitous apple, or even sharp plums.

In with the milk powder
At this point you can add:

Dry Spices
Dry spices need to be toasted to extract the essential oils from them and really release their true flavor, but they need to be moved continuously over high heat to prevent them from burning. This is why they go in with the milk powder. When deciding which spices to use, you have two paths you can follow:

- You can add small amounts of aromatic spices that enhance flavors already in the sauce. Great examples of these include ground cumin, coriander seed, fennel seed, powdered garlic and onion, juniper berries, and mustard powder.
- Adding small amounts of spices will not make the spice a main flavor but will act as an aromatic, adding an extra layer that is not overt but complementary to the overall flavor.
- Alternatively, you can you can create an amalgam of flavors that complement each other and the meat by making an overtly spice-based sauce. Pork works with myriad spiced-based sauces, including the obvious that are readily associated with pork such as Cajun and Creole. However, I find that a lot of dishes you would not readily associate with pork, such as tagine and curry, work amazingly well.

Hard Herbs

Hard herbs, like spices, need to be toasted to allow the essential oils to perfume your sauce properly. The term *hard herbs* doesn't refer directly to the toughness of the herb but to the fact that the flavorings are hard to extract. However, they tend to be pretty tough anyway.

These should be treated in the same way as dry spices, toasted but prevented from burning. Small amounts of herbs bring an extra layer of depth to your sauce, increasing the complexity as it hits your palate without actually being a strong flavor. This is the essence of using hard herbs in most cookery because they tend to be very pungent and will railroad your dish if overused. When using hard herbs with pork, stick to using them as background flavors in small quantities.

Hard herbs and spices

Great hard herbs to try include bay leaves (fresh bring a much more floral note), thyme, rosemary (in small quantities), juniper berries, and mace blades.

In with the tomato paste
At this point you can add:

Wet Ingredients

Wet ingredients cover any ingredient that is not liquid but still has a high water content. In general, wet ingredients do not need heat to activate them, because they tend to be ready-to-eat ingredients such as mustard, jellies, or already cooked-out spice pastes, but often applying a little fierce heat for a short time will improve their flavor, as it does with tomato paste. Things to try include mustards, yeast extract, red currant jelly, peanut butter (great in curry-style dishes), and spice pastes such as green curry paste or a Cajun paste if you're not using dry spices.

HOMEMADE VERSUS STORE-BOUGHT

If you are a beginner experimental chef, packet spice mixes are a great way to start playing with flavors, but it is worth studying the back of the packet to see what they contain. Without a doubt, a good homemade spice mix is far superior to that of a store-bought mix. It is well worth spending some time investigating and playing with spices, because not only do you get better results, but it is also far cheaper in the long run to buy spices individually than pre-mixed.

Soft herbs

Soft Herbs

Now is also the time to add soft herbs (herbs you treat softly to extract their flavors, although they also tend to be physically softer herbs such as sage, parsley, and cilantro) as a background flavor. If you wish to use them as a main flavor, save them and add them at the end, just before you serve your sauce, so they retain their lovely fresh flavor, which would be lost if added now.

If you are going to add soft herbs to finish the sauce, you should just add the stalks here and save the leaves for later. Adding the stalks to stocks and sauces is the best way to get some use out of them.

Herbs to try include sage, parsley, cilantro, basil, chives, and tarragon (which goes really well with smoked pork products).

In with the chicken stock
At this point you can add:

Rather than adding extra liquid to the mix in this section, substitute what you wish to add for the equivalent volume of chicken stock so that the volume of the cooking liquor remains the same. Pretty much any liquid can be substituted for the chicken stock in this recipe with varying degrees of success; sometimes the chicken stock can even be completely replaced.

The only rule you really have to consider when playing with the liquid content is that alcohol must be added first and reduced by half in the case of spirits and by about a tenth for every other type of alcohol before any other liquids are added. By reducing the alcohol, not only do you intensify the flavor but you also evaporate off a lot of the alcohol. This is essential because raw alcohol in food will come through in the flavor of your finished product and can also react with other ingredients, giving you undesired consequences.

Deglazing the pan can add flavor; try using brandy, calvados, sherry, tequila, rum, whiskey, or cider vinegar.

You can add any of the following at up to a 50:50 ratio with the chicken stock: tomato juice, fruit juices, coconut milk, white wine, red wine, cider, heavy cream, cola (just don't use diet), and root beer (don't use diet).

Liquid

Now you know when to add your ingredients and how to add your ingredients. However, I haven't told you exactly how much you should add. This is because it's a massively sliding scale affected by multiple factors. There is no hard and fast way to give you that information, but as long as you are sensible you can't go far wrong.

I've also avoided set flavor combinations because I really feel that everyone should play with their food: experimentation is a great way to have fun with your cooking while learning for yourself. However, I will to give you some basic principles to follow when getting creative, so you're not completely in the dark.

1. You can easily add more ingredients, but it's much harder to remove them.

2. Classic combinations are classic combinations for a reason.

3. Stick to a theme: if you're cooking a North African–style dish with dry aromatic spices and fruit, either whiskey or Parmesan cheese is unlikely to work.

4. Use your brain and you can't go far wrong. If you think it sounds bad when you say it out loud, it probably will be bad. For example, pork cooked in Cajun tomato sauce sounds good; pork cooked in apricot, tarragon, and tequila sauce sounds bad. It's simple.

5. Be sparing with strong flavors because they can ruin your dish.

6. Don't overcomplicate the flavors. In most cases, a cooking liquor should have, at maximum, three strong flavors.

7. Finally, and most important of all, start conservative if you're new to being creative. Keep it simple and go for combinations that you know work, and then vary them a little.

POT ROASTING EXPERIMENTS AT A GLANCE

STYLE	AROMATICS	MILK POWDER	TOMATO PASTE	CHICKEN STOCK	TO FINISH
CAJUN	Finely chopped bell peppers with diced tomato flesh and roasted chiles	Paprika, dried oregano, ground coriander, cayenne pepper, dried thyme, and cumin	Finely chopped parsley and cilantro stalks. Add some brown sugar.	Deglaze with bourbon, add a splash of malt or cider vinegar, and replace half the chicken stock with tomato juice.	Finely chopped parsley and cilantro, and use cornstarch to thicken.
CHINESE	Fresh ginger, lemon grass, and chiles	Cinnamon, fennel seed, Sichuan pepper, star anise, and cloves (be really careful with the last two because they are very strong).	Soy sauce, honey, and fish sauce (this is really salty, so be careful).	As per usual. But, if you wish to make a sweet, sticky sauce, you can replace half the chicken stock with cola.	Use cornstarch to thicken and finish with plenty of slices of scallion. If making a cola-based sticky sauce, thicken it by reducing the liquid over high heat as your meat rests.
CIDER AND APPLE	Cooking apples	As per usual	Do not use tomato paste. Add sage leaves and a small amount of whole-grain mustard.	Add a large amount of medium dry hard cider to the pan and reduce by half. Use this to replace half of the chicken stock.	Finish off the sauce by adding finely chopped eating apples and parsley.
CHASSEUR	As per usual	As per usual	Tarragon and parsley stalks	Add precolored lardons of smoked bacon or pancetta, then deglaze the pan with a healthy glug of white wine.	Add sautéed mushrooms 15 minutes before the end of cooking and finish the sauce with plenty of chopped tarragon and parsley.
MOROCCAN	Finely chopped fennel	Cayenne, black pepper, paprika, turmeric, cinnamon, chopped apricots, and chopped dates	Dash of honey and chopped tomatoes.	Replace half the chicken stock with tomato juice.	Add almond slices, cubed dried apricots, and chopped parsley and cilantro.
SPANISH	Chopped red bell pepper	Fennel seed, a pinch of turmeric, and plenty of thyme and smoked paprika	Chopped tomatoes	Replace one-fourth of the stock with tomato juice and another half with red wine.	Add plenty of roughly chopped green and black olives 20 minutes before the end of cooking and finish the sauce with diced red bell pepper and roughly chopped parsley.
BARBECUE	As per usual	Chipotle chiles, cinnamon, mace, smoked paprika, allspice, and mustard powder	Honey, soy sauce, Worcestershire sauce, a small amount of molasses, and a healthy amount of brown sugar	Deglaze the pan with a healthy splash of bourbon, add a splash of malt vinegar, and reduce, adding the full complement of chicken stock on top.	Don't thicken the sauce with anything while your meat is resting, then put the sauce in a pan, and reduce the liquid over high heat.

Chinese glazed pork belly

Signature Dish: Chinese-Glazed Pork Belly

Now that you have come to the end of the kitchen cooking section I'm going to share with you this really special dish of glazed pork belly. Unlike the other signature dishes, this one requires precision and exact measurements to get this flavor-packed dish right.

SERVES 6

INGREDIENTS

2¹/₂ pounds (1.13 kg) skinned belly pork
2 pig trotters,* split in half
Sesame oil, for sautéing
11 ounces (311 g) onions
11 ounces (311 g) celery
4 large cloves garlic
1 large knob fresh ginger
2 stalks lemon grass
3 fresh mild chiles
1 tablespoon (8 g) milk powder
1¹/₂ sticks cinnamon
2 teaspoons fennel seed
2¹/₂ teaspoons Szechuan pepper
1¹/₂ star anise
4 cloves
3 heaped tablespoons (32 g) tomato purée
5 tablespoons (75 ml) soy sauce
5 tablespoons (100 g) honey
2 teaspoons fish sauce
1 cup (235 ml) orange juice
Chicken stock, as required

* Trotters are optional but highly advisable because the gelatin from the trotter is what provides the extra viscosity to the sauce that will cause it to stick to and glaze the meat properly.

1. WASH, DRY, AND REFRIGERATE THE MEAT UNTIL READY TO USE.
See page 34.

2. ROAST THE TROTTERS.
Preheat the oven to 360°F (185°C), place the trotters in a pan, and roast until golden brown.

Roasting trotters

3. SEAL THE MEAT.

In a hot pan, sear the meat until it is colored enough that it looks like a finished piece of roast pork.

4. PREPARE THE LIQUID.

In a pan over medium-high heat, sauté the onions, celery, garlic, ginger, lemon grass, and chiles in sesame oil for 1 minute.

Add the milk powder, cinnamon, fennel seed, Szechuan pepper, star anise, and cloves to the mix and continue to sauté until the onions start to lightly brown.

Add the tomato purée, soy sauce, honey, and fish sauce, and cook for 1 minute, stirring continuously.

Place the meat in the pan and pour in the orange juice and enough chicken stock to cover it entirely.

Add the roasted trotter to the sauce, making sure that you deglaze the roasting pan at the end to get all of its meaty flavor.

5. COOK THE MEAT.

Lower the oven temperature to 220°F (105°C) and insert your in-oven temperature probe (if you have one). Place a lid on your pan, put it in the oven, and cook until the core temperature of your meat has reached 170°F (75°C).

6. PREPARE THE GLAZE.

Remove the meat from the cooking liquid, transfer to a plate to rest, and turn your oven up to 450°F (230°C, or gas mark 8).

Strain the cooking liquid into a saucepan and reduce to half over high heat, using a spoon to skim any fat and scum from the top. Continue reducing the liquid until it is the consistency of maple syrup.

7. PREPARE THE ROASTING PAN.

Line a roasting pan with tinfoil, pour in water to ¼ inch (6 mm), and place metal trivets (a cake cooling rack will do) on the tinfoil. This will prevent any excess glaze from burning to the pan.

Glaze ready to use

Glazing the meat

8. GLAZE THE MEAT.

Once your meat has rested properly, cut it into portions and place them on the trivets, ensuring that they aren't touching one another. Then, using a pastry brush, paint a generous coating of the glaze all over the meat. Drizzle 1 teaspoon of the glaze to the top of each portion and immediately place the tray into the oven. Allow the meat to sit in the oven for roughly 2 to 4 minutes.

Remove the tray from the oven and apply another teaspoon of glaze to the top of your meat. Repeat this process three to six times until a glossy, thick, and sticky coat of the glaze has formed on the meat.

CHEF'S TIPS

When glazing, you need to keep your eyes on the meat, because 2 minutes is only a rough guide to the timing. If the glaze starts to blacken and burn, it's done regardless of time. Equally, if the glaze has not gone tacky and stuck to the meat, you need to allow the glaze to dry for a little longer and turn your oven up a little.

9. SERVE THE MEAT.

Remove the pan from the oven, transfer the meat to a plate, and let rest for 10 minutes. The meat with the glaze should be moist enough to serve without any extra sauce. However, if you wish to serve a little sauce with your meat, try adding a little orange juice and zest to the remaining liquid to turn it into a fantastic accompaniment.

This is a really special dish that looks great and will always visually wow anyone you serve it to. However, it really comes alive when its aroma enters the vicinity of your nostrils. The rich, meaty smell of the roasted pork laced with the wafting perfume of the aromatic oriental spices really sets the mouth watering. And the taste—it's indescribable!

Of all the signature dishes in this book, this is really the most exceptional. If executed well, the dish that you will serve will sit comfortably on the table at the most prestigious of restaurants despite the fact that this is a really inexpensive cut. This is the art of being a good chef: taking a much underutilized cut and making it better than a prime cut with love and attention. This dish will take a long time to make in the cooking sense, but hands-on preparation is not really that long.

However, the best thing about it is that you can pot roast the belly, portion it up, and make the glaze a couple of days in advance. Then, when required, simply heat the pork up slowly in some chicken stock a few hours before eating. Then apply the glaze, stir-fry some pak choi, quickly assemble, and dazzle the guests of any party without even breaking a sweat.

Now that you have mastered the art of home roasting pork it's time to go the whole hog. You might think that this is where the book ends for you, because roasting a whole pig is difficult and hard work. However, you couldn't be more wrong. Over the last several chapters, you've learned almost all the skills you will need, and it actually is really easy. However, do keep that to yourself or you won't be revered by all as the king or queen of pork.

Dinner Party Shortcut

You can use a temperature probe to keep the cooking liquid to about 149°F (50°C) once the core temperature of the meat has reached 140°F (°C). In this way, you can keep your meat on hold for a good few hours (until required) without causing much detriment to the quality of the meat.

Finished meat

CHAPTER 6

Roasting a Whole Hog ★★★★★

Roasting a whole hog is simple. It's just like roasting one of the smaller joints, and the same principles apply. Tougher cuts need slower cooking, and tender cuts need less heat or they will start to dry out. You can brine, marinate, rub, and glaze to your heart's content by scaling up the techniques you've already learned.

In short, if you know how to control the heat on your barbecue and have worked your way through the previous sections of the book, roasting a whole pig will be easy. This section will run you through the most popular method—classic spit roast—and how to do it to perfection. Then just in case you want something even easier and quicker we take a quick look at the highly ingenious Caja China.

THREE BASIC CATEGORIES OF BARBECUE METHODS:
1. THE LAZY WAY
Buying prepackaged salads and meat and slinging it on the grill. This is great for an impromptu event or gathering but will never really wow anyone invited.

2. THE STYLISH WAY
Serving home-marinated quality meat and sumptuous burgers and bratwursts accompanied by lovely fresh salads with homemade dressings and sauces. This will impress everyone you invite and will have a great wow factor.

3. GOING WHOLE HOG
Roasting a whole pig, taking time to lovingly and slowly cook the flesh to perfection as the pig emanates smells that will make every meat eater in your area salivate. All this while sipping the tipple of your choice while other people do all the running around for you because they honestly think what you're doing is hard.

If you really want to wear the crown of barbecue king or queen, and create awesome summer memories, read on.

Roasting a hog

Hog on spit roast

Spit Roasting a Whole Hog

The rotisserie style of cooking has been around as long as humans have been cooking over fires and in the past has been used to cook things as large as whole cows. The rotation during cooking is very important to this method for several reasons, the first obviously being the even distribution of heat over the meat. The second and less obvious is that the rotation causes the meat to baste itself during the cooking process, thus helping to keep the meat moist.

PROS

- Way cheaper to feed a lot of people compared to a regular barbecue or a buffet
- Can use gas if you're not great with fire
- Complete control over distribution of heat by controlling the amount of coal or the intensity of the burner under each area, allowing you to slow cook tough areas and quick cook tender ones
- Looks really impressive
- Makes awesome crackling
- Can constantly monitor the heat in all areas of the pig
- Takes a long time to cook, so takes on a smoky flavor
- Causes the meat to constantly self-baste

CONS

- Sudden heat spikes from flare-ups can burn crackling
- Really difficult to do in windy or rainy conditions
- Takes much longer than the Caja China method (see pages 136–137)
- Once the crackling is ready, you will have to fight ravenous guests to prevent them from tearing chunks off before the meat is ready

Where to Get a Hog

Sourcing a whole pig is not difficult; you just have to decide what type of pig you want. But, if you are going to roast a whole hog, it is worth spending a little more money for a great pig—quality pork really shines through.

Locating a supplier is very easy. Contact your nearest butcher and have him or her order a pig for you: simple as that. This should be done at the very minimum a week in advance to give your butcher the time to source exactly the right size pig for you and allow it time to arrive.

If you don't have a local butcher or cutting plant, log onto www.eatwild.com. This is a directory of local farmers who will sell you a whole pig directly, allowing you to shop from the farm. Buying direct can also save you money, especially if you live in a city (I have been quoted 150 percent over the base price of a pig by one city butcher).

How Much Hog Do I Want?

This is probably the easiest thing to remember in the whole book. When buying a whole hog for roasting you need to order 2 pounds (905 g) of meat (not including the weight of the head) per person. Really, it is that simple, and you don't have to worry about the weight of the head because whoever you are ordering from will be able to accurately guesstimate the weight of a pig without the head for you.

Once cooked and removed from the bones, this will provide roughly 8 ounces (225 g) of meat per person. But, when ordering meat, it is always best to get a few extra portions to ensure that everyone can eat his or her fill and you can still have some meat remaining for sandwiches the next day (or my favorite: pulled pork and coleslaw in flat bread).

What Do I Ask for When I Order?

To order a pig for spit roasting, simply ask for a whole dressed pig in the weight you require. It is up to you whether you wish to have the head on or off. But, by removing it you are missing out on the amazing pig cheeks that will have confit in their own fat, making them succulent, flavorful, and definitely one of the best pieces of meat in your roast.

The Equipment

When you are going to cook a whole pig, most of the basic tools required will already be sitting in your kitchen, although you will probably have to buy a couple of tools to complete the kit. This, coupled with the fact that you can rent both Caja China boxes and spit-roasting setups, means that trying a whole hog roast for the first time need not be expensive.

As long as you have the essential equipment laid out in this section you will have everything you need to get the job done. Don't get me wrong; I love gadgets, but most of the barbecue gadgets that are out there can be replaced with everyday kitchen items that do the job just as well.

PIG TOO BIG?

If you find your pig is a little too big for your roaster, remove the bottom of the legs and the head. Use a sharp heavy knife like a cleaver and a sterilized hacksaw to cut through the bones and, 20 minutes of gory film re-enactment later, it'll fit.

Some of the tools you'll need

Tools and Basic Utensils

Disposable razor

Temperature probe with a heat-resistant cable (I)

Clean and sterile prep table large enough
to fit your whole hog on

Food-safe sanitizer

Thick oven mitts (you will be handling
scorching hot metal)

Tongs (G)

Slide-out utility knife (B)

Kitchen shears (C)

Boning knife

Meat fork (F)

Sharp kitchen knife (E)

Knife sharpener (D)

Refrigerator large enough to fit your hog in

Roll of 16-gauge (or higher) steel wire

Pliers with wire-cutting tool

Large disposable aluminum pans or trays

Metal bin suitable for disposing of ash as you cook (A)

When Using Charcoal as a Heat Source

Second set of tongs to move coals (J)

Small metal shovel (suitable for removing
ash and moving coals) (K)

Spray bottle filled with water

Well Worth It, but not Essential to Have

Latex disposable gloves

Apron

Kitchen Towels (H)

Charcoal versus Gas

Charcoal or gas is an argument that has been going on in the barbecue world since the first gas grills and barbecues were made. It's not an argument I wish to get in the middle of (but if you wish to laugh at grown men and the occasional woman slinging bile, look up some of the forums on the subject and you will see why I don't wish to get involved). However, there is a new kid on the block in the hog-roasting world that both sides rail against: the electric grill. I would love to take a couple of pages to fully dissect the subject of the heat source but I have been told that it's incredibly boring when I talk about it so I'm not going to make you read it all; instead, I will give you a short rundown to help you make your own decision.

Ease of Use

The best way of thinking about this is how easily you can control the heat levels emitted from your heat source. The clear winners of this are the gas and the electric units because you have complete minute-by-minute control over the heat that is emitted at the turn of a dial. These two cookers also have the benefit that they don't cause flare-ups from the dripping fat, thus giving a more even heat. Despite this, it is not at all hard to control a charcoal burn if you have a basic knowledge of fire tending; it just requires more work. Solid wood is by far and away the hardest method to control, giving the least even heat and burn rate, so only really experienced roasters should try it.

Practicality

This boils down to how readily you will be able to use your grill if you buy one. The clear winners of this are the gas and electric units, because both entail simply firing up the grill and being ready to cook in a matter of minutes, whereas with charcoal you need to prepare your fire at least 20 minutes prior to cooking. This means you are far more likely to get more use from gas and electric grills due to the ability to come home from work and roast a whole chicken or joint of meat for dinner almost as quickly as if you used your oven.

Taste

It has been shown that there is little difference in flavor between meats quickly cooked over barbecues and flame grills. However, the long, slow cooking of a hog over solid fuels (charcoal and wood) really imparts a lovely smoky flavor to the meat. This adds a gorgeous complexity to the flavor of your end-product, making wood and charcoal the clear choice if taste is your goal.

Cost

Now this can be broken down in to two categories: cost of the unit and cost to run said unit. When looking at the cost of the unit, solid fuel barbecues really are the clear winner. You can purchase a complete solid fuel barbecue for around a tenth of the price of a gas unit, and electric setups are monstrously expensive. You can look online and find really simple guides to show you how to build your own solid fuel setup for even less.

When we look at the actual cost of day-to-day running the unit, gas and electricity are the clear winners, costing less than a third in fuel per burn than their solid fuel counterparts.

Unless you are a hard-core roaster and intend to really use and abuse your grill, the solid fuel grills are the way forward if you are looking to keep the cost down. Yes, they cost more to run, but it is highly unlikely that you will recoup the extra expense of a gas or an electric grill in the money saved in fuel costs over its lifetime. If you do wish to use gas or electric for your hog roast, it is most likely to be more cost-effective to rent one.

Safety

There are some genuine concerns that should really be taken into consideration when choosing which type of grill to get. We're not talking about which ones are the most likely to blow up in your face but which ones are practical in terms of safety considerations.

If you have a nice large space to roast in, this section does not really apply to you as long as you roast away from buildings and make sure that nothing above you is going to burst into flames. However, if you do have limited space, such as a balcony or a roof terrace, open fires near buildings are completely out of the question. This leaves you with two options: go somewhere else where you have the space, or use an electric rotisserie.

The downside of this is that you will not be able to roast a whole pig (an electric grill that size is prohibitively expensive unless you can find somewhere to rent one), but if you're limited in space you probably won't have enough people to finish all the meat of a whole pig anyway.

Fuel for Your Fire

By now, you should have figured out which fuel type you wish to use and purchased or rented you equipment. The next question you need to answer is how much fuel you will need to complete your hog roast. This is easy. For an electric grill, just plug it in and you have an endless source of heat. For gas, wood, and charcoal grills, use the following chart.

WEIGHT OF PIG	CHARCOAL	GAS	WOOD	ESTIMATED BURN TIME
Up to 80 pounds (36.4 kg)	75 pounds (34 kg)	30 pounds (13.6 kg)	¼ cord	6–7 hours
80–110 pounds (36.4-50kg)	85 pounds (38.6 kg)	35 pounds (15.9 kg)	⅓ cord	7–8 hours
110–130 pounds (50-59kg)	95 pounds (43.2 kg)	40 pounds (18.2 kg)	½ cord	8–9 hours

The above figures are rough estimates. I would advise getting a little more to ensure that you are not making a fuel-run halfway through cooking.

How to Spit Roast a Pig

When you embark on the satisfying journey of hog roasting, you are following in the footsteps of our ancestors, cooking in a way that has been used all over the world since the dawn of time. Many people think that roasting in front of an open fire is a primitive and dirty cooking method. Nothing could be further from the truth; it is a highly controlled and sophisticated procedure with an advanced science behind it (okay, cavemen probably didn't know this, but penicillin, the pacemaker, and cola were all discovered by accident) that yields fantastically flavorful meat. This process can be adapted to roasting pretty much anything you wish as long as it will fit on your spit, from smaller cuts of meat to some things you really wouldn't expect. Among the most unusual things I have seen are a spit full of roasted lobsters and pineapples roasted with a whole pig, both of which were smoky and exquisite.

WHAT SORT OF CHARCOAL TO USE

If you are using charcoal as your fuel source, only use lump wood charcoal. Never briquettes because they will not give you the heat needed to scorch the skin in the hot flash stage, and throughout your burn you will need to remove the ash continually or it will choke your fire.

Preparing the Pig

By now, you should have ordered your pig. The day before the roast, follow these steps. Also get the tools and the fuel in place the day before and you'll be set and raring to go.

1. SHAVE YOUR PIG.

Using a disposable razor, remove any hair that remains on the pig. This sounds a little gross, but what is worse: eating burnt hair–flavored crackling or shaving a pig? You decide.

2. WASH YOUR PIG.

Rinse the meat clean to ensure that any hair is removed. With a whole pig, you probably won't be able to do this in the sink. Methods I've used have included hanging a pig from a tree and using the garden hose and washing it in the bath, although I also know someone who took his pig in the shower once. Whichever way you do this, you need to ensure that you have thoroughly sanitized the area before and after you wash your meat.

3. DRY YOUR PIG.

Pat your pig dry with paper towels. Removing surface moisture will enable the salt rub to work more effectively, resulting in better crackling.

4. SCORE THE CRACKLING.

Using your utility knife, score the skin of the pig a uniform 1 inch (2.5 cm) between horizontal scores (nose to tail); for the vertical scores (leg to leg), score every 2 inches (5 cm).

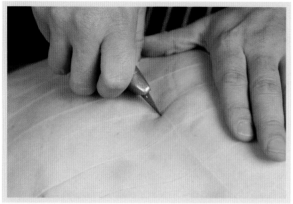

4. Scoring the crackling

5. APPLY THE CRACKLING RUB.

Apply the crackling rub (pages 35–36) all over the skin, ensuring that you force the mixture into each one of the scores. This is the same as with roasting smaller joints and is the key preparation step for getting great crackling.

6. STORE YOUR MEAT OVERNIGHT.

Wrap your meat and put it in the fridge overnight. This sounds really simple, but have you ever tried

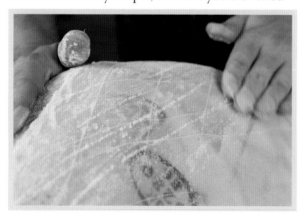

5. Rubbing the pig

to store a 30- to 100-pound (13.7 to 45.5 kg) floppy item in your fridge? I didn't think so. The most important thing is that, if possible, it needs to go in your fridge uncovered to allow the moisture to escape the fat and dry out the meat.

If you can't fit your pig in the fridge you are at a bit of a roadblock. Ideally, you should look into borrowing someone else's fridge space for the night. However, when forced to, I have stored my pig packed in ice in the bathtub.

If your pig will be packed in ice in the bathtub, you need to wrap it to prevent the ice from wetting the crackling rub and prevent it from doing its work. This is best done with plastic wrap. Completely wrap your rubbed meat, trying to keep as much of the salt mix in place as you do this. You need to ensure that you have enough ice to fill your bath with the pig in it. I know this is a lot of ice, but throwing away a bath full of ice is cheaper than throwing away a whole pig.

To fill the tub with ice, pull the plug out of the bath to allow ice melt to escape. Fill the bath one-fourth of the way with ice. Place the pig in your bath as it would stand, nestling the pig into the ice so that it will stand up; make sure the level of the pig's back is well below the level of the bath. Add the rest of your ice around and over the pig, making sure that the entire pig is covered. If the air temperature of your bathroom is quite warm, cover the tub with a waterproof layer, such as a tarp, then with a blanket or two to help insulate the pig and ice. I strongly advise checking how much ice has melted just before you go to bed and fill it up as appropriate. Finally, pray that the ice keeps your pig under 40°F (5°C).

Cooking the Pig
You'll need to get up early if you're cooking for lunch. Allow an hour for preparation, and plan on 90 minutes of cooking time per 10 pounds (4.5 kg) of pig.

1. REMOVE YOUR PIG FROM STORAGE AND RINSE.
Use the method you used previously to rinse your pig, ensuring that you remove all the crackling rub, and then pat your meat dry with paper towels. Cover your pig in a cool, shaded place for an hour or two to allow the meat to come to room temperature. This helps the meat cook more evenly because the center of the pig will take less time to come to a safe temperature. You should limit this period to two hours because any longer and you allow time for pathogens to multiply on your meat and thus creating a health hazard.

2. SEASON YOUR PIG.
Generously season your pig with salt all over and rub it into the skin and the meat. If you wish to add a spice rub, do so now. See page 144–146 for recipes and suggestions.

3. GET YOUR FIRE READY.
If you are using gas, you may think you can skip this step, but don't; you don't have to burn up a lot of gas, but just check that everything is working to avoid a nasty surprise. If you are using charcoal, start this process 30 minutes (solid wood, 1 hour) before it is time to start cooking your pig. For this I am assuming that you know how to light charcoal (especially because you can get self-lighting coal that only requires a couple of matches to get it burning).

Figure out, when the pig will be mounted on the spit, where the shoulder and the hams will be in relation to your fire. At each of these two points place a pile of about 5 pounds (2.3 kg) of charcoal. Light these piles to allow them time to get going properly.

4. MOUNT YOUR PIG.
Place your hog on the table with its spine at the top, its front legs stretched out in front of it, and its

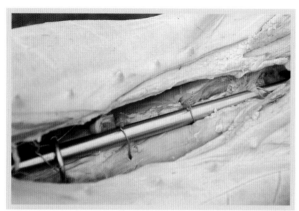

4. Pig with spit through it

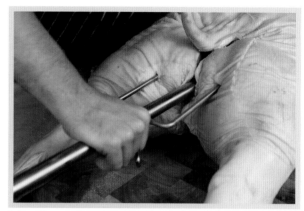

5. Pig with prongs through cheeks

back legs stretched out behind. Place your spit pole in through the mouth and out through the anus.

Place the first fork on the back end of the pole, with the spikes facing into the pig, and push the prongs into the center of the hams. You need to make sure they are as close to the middle of the ham as possible because this will give them the best grip and will also help conduct heat to the middle of the hams, speeding their cook time.

5. PRONG THROUGH THE CHEEKS.

Place the second fork on the pole at the head end and push the prongs into the cheek fat if you have a pig with the head on, or into the center of the shoulder meat if there is no head. This is the same as with the prongs in the hams but you need to push these prongs pretty tight to the pig because during cooking the pig will shrink and you may find your forks are not as effective at gripping the meat.

6. SECURE THE FEET.

Stretch the front feet out in front of the pig and use the leg braces that came with your spit roaster or wire them to the spit so that they are pulled out in front of the carcass and not hanging down. Do the same with the back feet. This opens up what is, for use of a better term, the armpit of the pig and helps the heat penetrate into the shoulder more evenly. Also, this keeps the weight close to the center of the spit, which will put less pressure on the forks so that your pig will be far less likely to twist and fall from the spit.

7. FASTEN TIGHT.

Turn your pig upside down so that you can see the inside of the pig and the bar running along its spine. Using your thin-bladed boning knife, punch a hole on either side of the spine (but as close to it as possible) all the way through the flesh and out the other side. Then thread the steel wire through the holes and around the bar and cut the

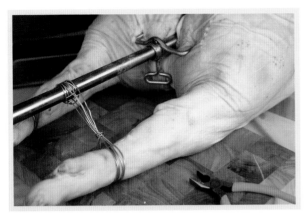

6. Securing pig feet

wire, leaving a U shape with at least 1½ inches (3.8 cm) of wire free at either end. Grab both ends of the wire with pliers and twist them together to complete the loop. Continue twisting the ends of the wire to tighten the loop until it cannot be easily moved but not so tight that it rips the skin and flesh. Repeat this every 8 inches (20.3 cm) all the way along the spine.

It is vitally important to secure the meat properly to the spit. Following all these steps thoroughly because as the meat comes to the end of its cooking time it will have tenderized immensely to the point when it will fall off the bone—and possibility fall off the spit into the fire pit.

8. CHECK THE HEAT.

Gas: Light the gas burners that will be under the hams and the shoulders and increase the heat until it is at the level that the meat will be and is scorching hot. Test this by putting your

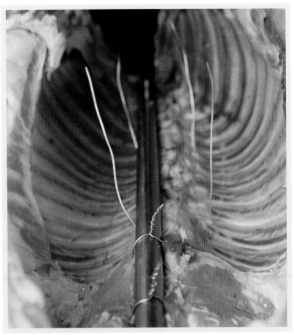

7. Completely wired pig

hand here: If you can hold your hand there for only a couple of seconds the temperature is about right.

Solid fuel: Check that there is plenty of heat coming from your two piles of coal by placing your hand the same distance from the heat that your meat will sit over the fire piles. If you can only hold your hand there for a few seconds, your fire is ready to start. If the heat is not quite scorching your hand after a couple of seconds, either mount your pig slightly closer to the fire or burn some more coal to increase the heat.

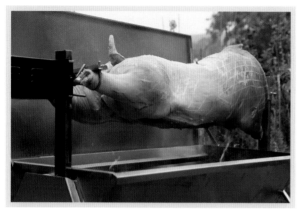
8. Test the flames

Just as with all the home-roasting methods we will color the meat for flavor and blister the skin in preparation for crackling using a hot flash. However, we will start cooking the hams and the shoulder (the tougher cuts) first to allow them extra time to tenderize (hence only having fire under these parts of the pig at the beginning).

9. HOT FLASH THE TOUGH CUTS.

Get someone else to help you with this. Place your spitted pig onto your roaster following the instructions that come with it and engage the motor. Allow the pig to spin with only the shoulders and hams over the fire until you see the skin starting to blister (about 5 to 10 minutes). The hot flash here has the same effect as during the other cooking processes in the book: It starts the flavor-boosting Maillard reaction going and scorches the crackling, causing it to start to bubble and making your crackling light and fluffy.

10. TURN DOWN THE HEAT.

Gas: Turn the heat down below the hams and shoulders to a gentle heat. You will know it is the correct heat if you can put your hand next to the pig and hold it there for approximately 5 to 7 seconds before you have to remove it.

Charcoal: Spread the piles of coal out so that none is directly below the pig, making a U shape of coals. Place one of your aluminum pans in the middle of each of the L shapes of coal to prevent them from falling back into the center and to catch any falling meat juice. The heat level should be the same as with the gas; you should be able to hold your hand next to the pig for 5 to 7 seconds before it gets too hot. During the whole cooking time you should strive to prevent any coal or other debris from falling into your foil pans because the juices collected will be used later to add extra flavor and moistness to your meat.

Once you have the heat to this level under your tougher ends of meat you need to maintain this temperature for the rest of the cooking process. This is easy with gas because you have temperature control at the twist of a dial. With solid fuel you have to keep an eye on the heat, adding coals or damping them down with your water spray to ensure you can maintain the correct level of heat. When adding coal, add just a little and often: this will provide a more even heat that is much easier to control.

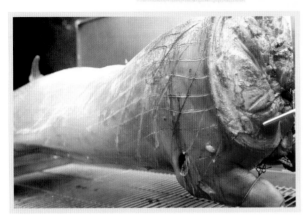

9. Scorched pig

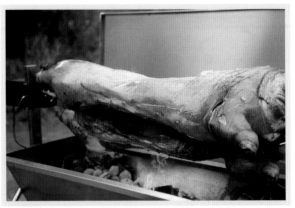

12. Starting to cook the center section

This is exactly the same as slow roasting because you are using a slow, gentle heat to cook the hams and shoulders through, trying to retain as much moisture as possible while aiming to get your core temperature to 175°F (80°C) to denature the collagen and break down the connective tissue, tenderizing the meat.

11. PREPARE TO HOT FLASH THE TENDER CUTS

Wait approximately one-third of your estimated cooking time before you start this step.

Gas: Skip this step.

Charcoal: At each end of your fire pit but not under the pig if you can, add an extra 6 to 8 pounds (2.7 to 3.6 kg) of charcoal to the fire, using the hot coals under the pig already to help ignite the charcoal. Wait until it is fully alight and kicking out plenty of heat before moving on.

By lighting the coals away from the middle of the pig you prevent it from starting off under a gentle heat, which will cause the crackling to dry out before it has a chance to blister, leaving you with tougher crackling.

12. HOT FLASH THE TENDER CUTS.

Gas: Light the burners under the middle of the pig and turn them up to the same scorching temperature used earlier on the hams and the shoulders.

Charcoal: Use a metal shovel to lift the extra burning coal that you have just started at each end into the middle of the fire pit and place directly under the pig. Leave the heat this high until the skin starts to scorch over the heat (roughly 5 to 10 minutes as with the tougher cuts).

13. DROP THE HEAT UNDER THE TENDER CUTS.

Gas: Turn the heat down to the same cooking temperature as the hams and the shoulders.

13. Spreading the coal to complete the circle

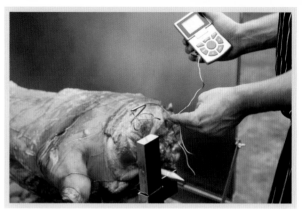

14. Temperature probe in nearly cooked pig

Charcoal: Push the charcoal to the side of the fire pit so you complete the two L shapes of coal at either end to make a U that is around the outside of the pig. Place more aluminum pans in the middle to catch the juices that fall during cooking. Try to maintain the same cooking temperature at the head and tail ends (5 to 7 seconds before you have to remove your hand).

The hard work for now is done. All you have to do now is sit back and enjoy, every now and then checking the heat levels under the pig and adjusting the burner strength if using gas or adding coal or damping the fire if using charcoal.

14. MAINTAIN TEMPERATURE CONTROL.

About three-quarters of the way through our estimated cooking time you should start monitoring the core temperature of the meat with your temperature probe. You are looking for two different core temperatures. Over the shoulders and hams you want a core temperature to reach 175°F (80°C) for at least 30 minutes. For the loin and belly you want your meat to reach a core temperature of 145°F (63°C).

If you feel that one area is going to be ready before the other, you should lower the heat under this area to allow the others to catch up. For gas, this is easily done by turning down the burners. With charcoal you need to remove some coals and use your spray bottle to damp down the remaining coals to reduce the heat and slow the cooking.

This is the true art of spit roasting a pig to perfection: getting the tender loin and belly meat to be ready at the same time as the tougher hams and shoulders, and it is something that will probably take a couple of roasts to do. But if you get it right, you will end up with juicy but firm meat from the loin and belly, and tender pulled pork from the shoulders and hams.

Once your meat has reached the desired temperatures and has been thoroughly checked with your temperature probe you are ready to remove your pig.

Serving Your Pig

1. REMOVE THE PIG FROM THE SPIT.

Get someone to help you with this. Ensure that you have enough dry oven mitts to be able to handle the spit and that you have a clean table for the pig cleared and ready to use.

Lift the pan of juices from the bottom of the fire pit and place them in a line on your pig table. Follow the manufacturer's instructions for releasing the spit bar, then, using oven mitts, lift the spit free and carry your pig to the table, laying it down on the juice pans so that all the juices are collected.

2. LET THE PIG REST.

Cover your pig in clean dish towels and allow the pig to rest for a minimum of 45 minutes but ideally until the core temperature of the loins reaches 130°F (50°C).

3. BREAK DOWN YOUR PIG.

Break the pig down into thirds, removing the hams and the shoulder meat from the loin section.

To do this, use a sharp knife to cut through the meat just in front of the hip joint of the hams and just behind the shoulder blade for the shoulder. The meat should be nice and tender and cut really easily. The only problem you might have is parting

1. Pig being lifted from spit

the spine. This is quite easy: all you need to do is find a gap between the vertebrae and cut through the soft tissue there.

Breaking down the pig separates the different meats; the meat of the shoulders and hams that is great for pulling and the meat from the tender cuts that is great for carving into slices.

4. PULL THE TOUGH CUTS.

Remove the bone from the hams and shoulders; this should be easy because the meat has become so tender that it falls away from the bone with a gentle pull. Then, using either two forks or your hands (use two or three latex gloves layered up if using hands), literally pull the meat into roughly bite-size chunks. Put the pulled meat into a warm serving dish and add all the cooking juices that you collected in the aluminum pans and toss together. Allow this mix to stand in a warm place while you carve your tender meat and it will be ready to serve.

5. CARVE THE TENDER CUTS.

Now that the shoulder section has been removed from the center section of the pig, you will be able to open up the pig by spreading the rib cage out so that it will sit flat on the table, back side up, making the carving process much easier. Remove the crackling from the pig. This should be easy because the fat behind the meat will have melted and should come away with the slightest persuasion of a sharp knife. If any of your crackling has failed to crackle, cut this away from the bits that have with some kitchen scissors. Put this back on the grill with any of the failed crackling from the hams and shoulders to crisp. But be careful because this will burn really quickly, so keep a close watch.

Roast potatoes under the pig

DON'T WASTE THOSE COALS

If you remove your spit bar you can have fun with what's left of the fire because it's pointless to waste good coals. Try spit roasting some random stuff. I like pineapples or a whole chicken for tomorrow's lunch. A couple of lobsters to feed any of the pescatarians always amuses and goes down well as long as you clean your spit first.

6. REMOVE THE LOIN.

Now that the skin has been removed, the two long loin muscles should be visible. Starting at the head end, use your knife to cut through the meat all the way down to the ribs, about ¼-inch (6 mm) away from the loin muscle all along its length. Be careful once you have cut over the thirteen ribs; the knife will slip all the way through the meat because there are no more ribs in the last one-third of the pig.

7. CUT ALONG THE BACKBONE.

Then, starting at the head, run your knife along the entire length of the backbone, making an incision with the tip of your knife about ½-inch (1.3 cm) deep all the way along the backbone. You want to get your knife as close to the backbone

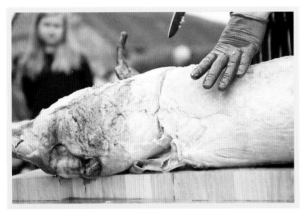

4. Separating the sections

5. Removing crackling

6. Removing the loin muscle

7. Last cut on separating the sections

as possible so that you get all the meat from the bone. To do this well and leave as little meat as possible on the bone, you should angle the cutting edge of the knife 2 to 3 degrees into the bone. If you get the right angle, the knife should slide along the bone, thereby wasting very little meat.

Now, use your fingers to pull the incision you made open a little so you can see how far you have cut. Using the tip of the knife, start to free the loin from the bone using little pressure on the knife to make long, stroking cuts. Continue this process until you meet the cut you made on the other side of the loin muscle and you have freed the meat Repeat this process to remove the other loin from the carcass and put both out of the way before the next step.

8. CARVE THE LOIN.

Bring your loin of pork back to the table and use a sharp carving knife to carve into slithers or steaks. Place on warmed plates or bowls.

9. PULL THE BELLY.

The belly of the pig will by now be melt-in-the-mouth soft and really juicy due to the large fat deposits throughout and the innate tenderness of the flesh itself. You can easily run a knife along the ribs to free the entire belly section. Once this has been removed it's a simple case of pulling the meat and adding it to the bowl with the other pulled meat.

7. Making an incision in the exposed spinal column

10. SERVE.

Yell, "Pig's ready!" and see how fast a whole pig can disappear.

Now you've successfully roasted a whole pig. It's time to sit back and enjoy the fruits of your labor and bask in the glory of continual praise. You are king or queen of the spit roast to all your friends and family.

SAVE THE BELLY

If you have plenty of meat for all your guests, the belly section of the pig is the best to reserve for a later date because it will stay the moistest and get the best results from reheating due to its high fat content.

8. Carving loin on board

9. Ready to serve

Spit Roasting Experiments

As with the other roasting techniques, both of the whole hog roasting methods can be messed around with to add flavor, moisture, and tenderness to your meat.

I like to emphasize the natural flavor of roast pork and rarely experiment with my pig if I'm cooking it for myself, allowing the natural juices, fat, and flavors caused by the Maillard reaction to be the signature flavor.

However, many people consider pork done this way bland (which probably means they are using low-quality lean pig that lacks natural flavor and under-seasoning the meat) and prefer to pack more flavor using spice rubs and the slightly clinical sounding but highly effective injection method, which combines marinating and brining without ruining your crackling.

Using Spice Rubs

When hog roasting, you apply the spice rub at two time points. Initially, you add a little of your spice rub to the crackling rub and apply this to the scored skin. At this point, you also use the spice rub alone to coat the cavity of the pig before leaving the pig in the fridge overnight; this allows the rub's flavor time to penetrate deep into the meat.

The second time occurs once you have rinsed your meat on the day of cooking and are applying your seasoning. First, you need to taste your spice rub. If it is already salty in taste, don't add any extra salt. However, if you can't taste salt add a little extra and mix it in until you get a hint of the salt's flavor coming through on your tongue. Once you have finished mixing your salt with your rub and you are ready to go, apply a thin coating of mustard to all the meat (not the skin) and rub your spice mix onto the mustard, which will act as a glue.

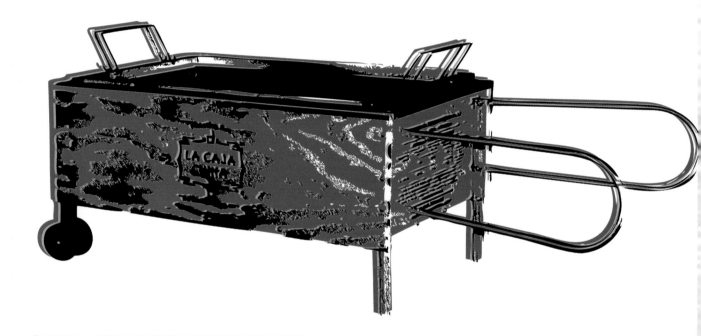

USING A CAJA CHINA BOX

Now before you rush out and go spit roast crazy, hold your horses for a second. There is another way that doesn't involve digging a hole, sticking it up a chimney, or anything more labor-intensive than buying a box. This is the Caja China, a traditional roasting method from Cuba.

The Caja China (Spanish for "Chinese box" but literally translated means "cleaver box") has become massively popular as of late since being bought over from Cuba. However, it has been around for a long time in the United States under the guise of the Cajun microwave and across Europe as the Dutch oven. This method of cooking is unusual because you place hot coals on top of the insulated box to create an oven effect.

PROS

- Cooks more quickly (20 to 40 percent faster) than other whole pig roasting methods
- No direct heat from flames preventing heat spikes from burning the skin
- Meat not falling into fire if improperly secured
- Works perfectly in bad weather as long as the coals keep burning
- Can easily roast joints of meat as well as whole pigs in the box
- Comes on wheels, so easily movable
- Keeps all the moisture in the box, so keeps the meat moister

CONS

- Only gets you pulled pork
- Quality of meat not as good as that of a spit roast
- Lacks the smoky hint of meat cooked over an open fire
- Most home use Caja China boxes limited to roasting 100-pound (45.5 kg) pigs or smaller
- Needs attachments to utilize the upward heat for grilling (but they are really cool)
- Keeps all the moisture in the box, so makes perfect crackling much harder to produce

In short, the Caja China is for you if you want to feed lots of people as quickly and easily as possible without worrying about serving perfection. That's not to say that a Caja China doesn't give great results, but its problem is that is cooks tough and tender cuts alike and the cracking is nowhere near as good as that from a spit roast. On top of this, the meat doesn't have the luscious smoked flavor of being cooked over an open fire, and unless you see it being cooked you would never know from the taste that it wasn't cooked in an oven. However, using a Caja China is so simple (the instructions are written on the side of the box) that you need no instructions on how to use it during the cooking stage.

What to Order

When ordering a pig for your Caja China box you need to ask for a butterflied whole pig. This means that the pig will come spilt through the middle with the skin of the back acting as a hinge.

How to Roast

Treat the butterflied pig exactly as you would for hog roasting. Score the skin, then apply the crackling rub and allow the rub to work overnight or as long as possible. Then simply follow the basic instructions that come with your box. For best results you should judge the doneness of your pork with an oven-safe probe. This should be placed in the center of the shoulder because it is the thickest part of meat. The pig is done when the core temperature reaches 175°F (80°C). It really is that simple.

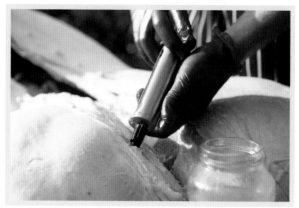
Injecting the pig

For a basic selection of spice rubs see pages 144–146; store-bought rubs are good too, just a little expensive.

Injecting

This is a really simple technique that involves using a flavor injector, which is basically a large hypodermic needle and syringe to inject the pork with brines and marinades. With both roasting methods brines and marinades should be injected as soon as the pig has been washed and dried, before you apply the crackling rub. Then let the pig sit for 10 minutes before patting it dry again and applying the crackling rub.

Juicy meat

Make your marinade or brine (see pages 146–147 for recipes). Fill your syringe with the mix and insert the needle into the center of the flesh. Inject the mix slowly; if the mix squirts back out you went too fast. Inject the pig all over, distributing the marinade evenly throughout the pig until it is all used.

IF BRINING, MIX UP 1$^{1}/_{2}$ QUARTS (1420 ML) BRINE PER 100 POUNDS (45.5 KG) OF PIG.

IF MARINATING, MIX UP 2 CUPS (475 ML) MARINADE PER 100 POUNDS (45.5 KG) OF PIG.

IF YOU WISH TO COMBINE BOTH, MIX UP 1$^{1}/_{2}$ QUARTS (1,420 ML) BRINE PER 100 POUNDS (45.5 KG) OF PIG, SUBSTITUTING 25 PERCENT OF THE BRINE WITH MARINADE.

This is a great way of using both marinades and brines, either separately or together, and still get crackling that crisps properly. You are effectively making your marinade or brine work from the inside out. The injected liquid sits in the pig overnight to penetrate the meat deeply, and it doesn't cost you an extra day of prep the way traditional brining and marinating do.

CHAPTER 7

Essential Pig-Roasting Experiments

As with the other roasting techniques, both whole roasting methods can be experimented with to add flavor, moisture, and tenderness to your meat by simply adding a few extra steps to basic preparation and the cooking method.

I like my roast emphasizing the natural flavor of roast pork and rarely play with my pig at all if I'm cooking it for myself. I allow the natural juices, fat, and the flavors caused by the Maillard reactions to be the signature flavor.

CRACKLING RUB

For every area of crackling the size of the palm of an average human hand, combine ½ teaspoon salt and ½ teaspoon baking soda.

However, many people consider pork done this way bland. This probably means they are using a low-quality, lean pig that lacks natural flavor and may be under seasoning the meat. More flavor is packed into the meat by using the techniques of spice rubbing, and the slightly clinical-sounding, but highly effective injection method, which combines marinating and brining without ruining the crackling.

Crackling being chopped on a board

Crackling

Apart from cooking it on the meat, there are three key methods for making crackling that you should know so that you can serve crackling with every pork dish you create. You can also just make crackling sometimes for an indulgent treat.

Crackling slab, chopped

Bowl of crackling

You will need to purchase a piece of back fat from your butcher with the skin still attached; they probably won't have this lying around, so you should order it at least a day in advance. The layer of fat under the skin should be roughly ¹/₂-inch (1.3 cm) thick, but if you ask them for a piece of skin to make crackling they will know what you're talking about.

Preparing the fat

Slabs of Crackling

Slabs of crackling are what I make if I'm going to serve a pot roast for a dinner party because it's quick and easy and can be used as an accompaniment. To prepare and crackle the skin, you simply treat it like the skin were still on the roast.

Score the skin every ¹/₂ inch (1.3 cm), making sure you don't cut all the way through.

Rub it with the crackling rub all over, forcing the mix into the slits. Leave it in the fridge overnight.

Preheat the oven to 480°F (240°C, or gas mark 9).

Rinse the mix off the skin and pat dry. Place it on a baking sheet. Cook for 10 minutes.

Lower the temperature to 350°F (180°C, or gas mark 4) and cook for 20 to 30 minutes longer.

This can be done in advance of any dinner and warmed through for 10 minutes in the oven before serving.

Rolling the skin

Rolled up skin

Crackling Nests

For this you will need to get much less fat on your skin, roughly ¼ inch (6 mm), and you need a really sharp kitchen knife.

Roll your sheet of crackling up into a sausage so that the fat is on the outside, secure in position using plastic wrap, and place in the freezer until set but not solid; an hour or so should do.

Remove from the plastic wrap and place on a chopping board. Use a sharp knife to slice the skin into matchstick-width disks. Season the now long strands with half the normal amount of cracking rub and place in the fridge overnight.

Rinse off the seasoning and allow to dry on a clean kitchen towel.

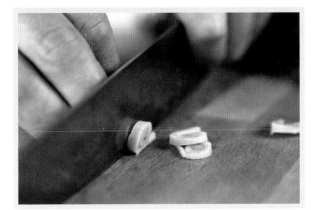
Chopping the skin

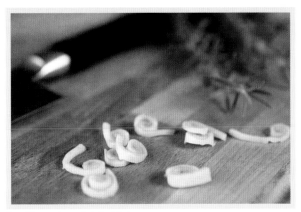
Crackling nests ready to be fried

Skin in strips on a baking sheet

When ready to cook, preheat a deep-fat fryer to 180°C (85°C) (if you don't have one use your temperature probe and a pan to create your own), add the crackling, and step back because it will start spitting at you. As soon as the crackling looks done, it is ready to be removed.

Drain the excess oil from the crackling and use it to make a fantastic dish look stunning.

Crackling Sticks

This is a great garnishing tool to make your dishes look fantastic when plating up.

Trim your cracking so that it has square edges. Slice the cracking into strips roughly $\frac{1}{3}$-inch (8 mm) wide. Place on a pan with and sprinkle with the crackling rub. Leave it in the fridge overnight.

Preheat the oven to 460°F (230°C, or gas mark 8).

Rinse and dry the crackling strips.

Get two identical baking sheets that fit together. Line one tray with parchment paper, cutting a duplicate of the piece used. Line up the strips on the baking pan, allowing $\frac{1}{2}$ inch (1.3 cm) between each and ensuring that the skin is facing up. Lay the second sheet of parchment paper on top and place the second tray on top. Weight the top with something that weighs 2 to 3 pounds (1 to 1.5 kg) that can go in the oven. Cook for 5 minutes.

Lower the temperature to 375°F (190°C, or gas mark 5) and cook for 10 minutes longer. If more time is needed, pour off the oil and return to the oven for 5 minutes longer.

Rubs

Spice rubs are a fantastic way to impart flavor to meat and once applied should be allowed to stand for a minimum of 3 hours to allow the flavors to permeate into the meat. Rubs come in two forms, wet and dry, and to be honest there is little difference between most wet rubs and their dry counterparts apart from the addition of a little liquid to a dry rub to make it a wet one.

A dry rub is made up of a blend of herbs and spices and can be either sprinkled over meat as a light seasoning or used in a large amount to add a highly flavored crust to your meat. A wet rub contains a liquid ingredient—usually oil and often vinegar—to form a paste to coat the surface of the meat, acting like a cross between a dry rub and a marinade.

Dry Rubs

Each of the following recipes makes roughly 1 cup of spice mix. When using the spice mix to strongly flavor and crust the meat, you should use 1 tablespoon of mix per pound (455 g) of meat.

All of these rubs should be made by simply combining all the ingredients, ensuring they are evenly mixed. The spice rub should be stored in an airtight container in a dry place and it will keep for up to 6 months.

These are a few of my favorite pork rubs, but really it's not hard to create your own to stunning effect. When playing with making your own rubs, it is really a matter of creating a flavor to suit your palate. As a start point, try editing the basic spice rub with a few flavors of your choice and work from there.

Basic Pork Rub

¼ cup (28 g) paprika
1 teaspoon cayenne
1 teaspoon chili powder
3 tablespoons (27 g) dry mustard
3 tablespoons (21 g) onion powder
3 tablespoons (27 g) garlic powder
2 tablespoons (9 g) ground basil
1 tablespoon (6 g) black pepper
1 tablespoon (18 g) salt
2 teaspoons (28 g) brown sugar for a sweet rub
2 extra teaspoons (5g) of both chili powder
　and cayenne for a hot rub

Kansas City Rub

½ cup (115 g) brown sugar
¼ cup (28 g) sweet smoked paprika
1 tablespoon (8 g) chili powder
1 tablespoon (9 g) garlic powder
1 tablespoon (7 g) onion powder
2 teaspoons (5 g) cayenne
1 tablespoon (6 g) black pepper
1 tablespoon (18 g) salt

Cajun Rub

2 tablespoons (14 g) smoked paprika
1 tablespoon (6 g) ground black pepper
1 tablespoon (7 g) ground cumin
1 tablespoon (15 g) brown sugar
1 tablespoon (18 g) salt
2 teaspoons (4 g) ground coriander
1 teaspoon (2 g) dried thyme
1 teaspoon (2 g) ground cayenne
½ teaspoon garlic powder
½ teaspoon ground allspice

Jamaican Jerk

3 tablespoons (21 g) onion powder
4 teaspoons (6 g) ground thyme
2 teaspoons (5 g) ground cinnamon
1 teaspoon (2.6 g) chili powder
1 tablespoon (9 g) garlic powder
4 teaspoons (16 g) sugar
2 teaspoons (12 g) salt
2 teaspoons (4 g) celery salt
1 teaspoon (4 g) ground allspice
2 teaspoons (13 g) black pepper

Chinese Spice Rub

¼ cup (22 g) ground ginger
¼ cup (24 g) ground Szechuan pepper
¼ cup (56 g) anise seed
2 tablespoons (7 g) red pepper flakes
2 tablespoons (14 g) ground cinnamon
2 tablespoons (13 g) ground cloves

Wet Rubs

Most wet rubs are simply dry rubs with a little oil and some acid such as vinegar or lemon juice added, so to create all the above as pastes, add a splash of oil and a dash of acid to turn them into wet rubs.

Harissa

12 whole dried red chiles (use medium
.....heat chiles unless you want it really hot)
3 cloves garlic, minced
½ teaspoon salt
2 tablespoons (30 ml) olive oil
1 teaspoon ground coriander
1 teaspoon ground caraway seed
½ teaspoon ground cumin

Soak the dried chiles in hot water for 30 minutes. Drain. Remove the stems and seeds. In a food processor, combine the chile peppers, garlic, salt, and olive oil. Blend. Add the coriander, caraway, and cumin and blend again to form a smooth paste. Store in an airtight container.

Thai Spice Paste

1 shallot, roughly chopped
1 stalk lemon grass
1 or 2 fresh red chiles
4 cloves garlic
1 thumb-size piece ginger, sliced
2 tablespoons (30 g) tomato purée
.....(fry this in a pan for a minute before adding)
1 teaspoon (3 g) ground cumin
¾ teaspoon (2 g) ground coriander
¼ teaspoon ground white pepper
2 tablespoons (30 ml) fish sauce

1 teaspoon (5 g) shrimp paste
1 teaspoon (4 g) sugar
1½ tablespoons (11 g) chili powder
3 tablespoons (45 g) thick coconut milk
2 tablespoons (30 ml) freshly squeezed lime juice

Throw it all in a blender and purée until smooth. Refrigerate in a sealed container.

Marinades and Brines

Marinades and really have an unlimited scope for you to play with and are simple to make as long as you know the base recipe. This is because once you have made the base recipe, you can pretty much flavor them with anything you want, most notably the spice mixes from the section above.

Basic Marinade

This basic marinade is enough to marinate a Boston butt (approximately a soccer ball size).

1 tablespoon (15 g) Dijon mustard
1 shallot
3 cloves garlic
2 tablespoons (30 ml) vinegar
.....or juice from a tart citrus fruit
2 cups (475 ml) oil
½ cup (120 ml) water

Place the mustard, shallot, and garlic in a blender and purée. Add the vinegar or citrus juice and blend again. Add the oil in a slow stream to the mix while the blender is running as if you were making a vinaigrette, then slowly add the water to the mix.

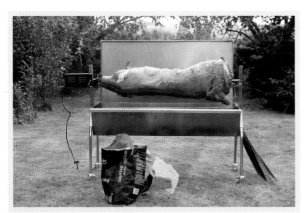
Meat drying on the rack

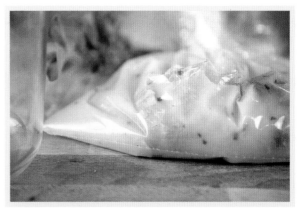
Meat in a marinade bag

Place the meat in a zipper-top bag, cover with the marinade, and marinate overnight.

To add flavoring to this marinade you can do one of three things:

1. Add 2 tablespoons (75 g) of dry rub in with the mustard, shallot, and garlic.

2. Add freshly chopped herbs right at the end just before marinating the meat.

3. Replace the ¹/₂ cup (120 ml) water with another strongly flavored liquid; pineapple juice, papaya juice, cider, and wine are all especially great because they contain enzymes that break down collagen, thus helping to tenderize your meat. Other things to try include beer, fruit juices, soy sauce (mixed 50:50 with water), or spirits such as bourbon, whiskey, or Calvados, but remember to cook out the alcohol first.

Basic Pork Brine

This recipe makes enough brine to cover a Boston butt (approximately the size of a soccer ball). Brined meat will become really moist and once cooked will be deliciously juicy and tender.

I gallon (4 L) cold water
¹/₂ cup (144 g) kosher salt (reduce to ¹/₄ cup [72 g] if using regular table salt)
²/₃ cup (150 g) light brown sugar
I cup (235 ml) cider vinegar
I tablespoon (5 g) black peppercorns
2 bay leaves

Combine all the ingredients in a large pan and heat over medium heat until the salt and sugar have dissolved, then allow to cool before brining the meat in the mix overnight.

To add flavor to this recipe, add I cup of spice rub to the ingredients when dissolving.

Gravy

Okay, sauce is a huge topic to cover and too big to do it justice properly. So I'm just going to show you how to convert your pan juices into a gravy. The basic method of making gravy from pan juices is very similar to making a cooking liquid for a pot roast and as such can be played with in the same manner (see page 105).

When your meat has finished roasting, use the juices that have leaked from the meat during cooking to help add flavor to the sauce that you are serving with the meat. Remove your meat and deglaze the pan, ensuring that any juice that is caramelized to the pan gets lifted off. (In general this will be done with white wine or stock, but any liquid that will work with your sauce will do.)

Then, in a saucepan, add any aromatics that you wish to use and sauté for about 1 minute. If you're not going to add any aromatics, just use a little chopped onion to prevent the pan from overheating and burning the gravy.

Gravy being poured

Chef's Idea

There are myriad great flavors that complement pork and make great gravy. Try adding apples and sage. Grate some apple in with the aromatics and sweat—just before serving, toss some finely shredded sage leaves to add a lovely, fresh floral note to the gravy.

Honey and mustard: Remove the tomato purée from the recipe and replace it with half the amount of mild Dijon mustard. Before adding your beurre manie, add a drizzle of honey to sweeten to taste.

Add caramelized onions and thyme. In a heavy-bottomed pan, caramelize some sliced onions in a hot pan and set aside. When adding the beurre manie to the gravy, add finely chopped thyme and the caramelized onions.

Next, add milk powder and any dried spices or hard herbs and fry for 1 minute.

Add tomato paste and any wet ingredients you wish to flavor the sauce with.

Pour the contents remaining in the tray into a saucepan, add chicken stock (homemade is best) to the pan liquor, and bring to a simmer. Simmer for as long as you rest for the meat.

Strain the liquid, and then thicken with beurre manié (page 104).

Conclusion

In short, this book can really be summed up with five essential tips (how depressing):

1. ALWAYS BROWN YOUR MEAT AND HOT FLASH YOUR CRACKLING.

2. GET A TEMPERATURE PROBE IF YOU WANT TO PREPARE PERFECT MEAT EASILY.

3. COOK TENDER MEATS TO A CORE TEMPERATURE OF 145^{8}F (63^{8}C).

4. COOK TOUGH CUTS AT 180^{8}F (85^{8}C) AND COOK UNTIL TENDERIZED.

5. AND, MOST IMPORTANT OF ALL, PLAY WITH YOUR FOOD AND EXPERIMENT; YOU STILL LEARN FROM DOING THINGS WRONG.

Unlike other books, this one really doesn't focus on teaching you specific recipes, but rather processes. Learning to cook dishes this way allows you to use them and transform them into so many more recipes. This isn't outside the box, but more making sure that you are aware of what's going on inside your food. For example, if you take the temperature probe technique in this book and apply it to cooking other meats, all you need to know are the correct core temperatures and away you go. If you continue to cook like this for a couple of years you start to see more complex overlapping principles and start extrapolating; this is when you will have started thinking like a chef.

I really believe in teaching cooking this way—it's like giving you a tool kit to allow you to play and create, and most important of all, have fun with your food.

Sitting dinner party

Resources

Suppliers

For every basic home cooking implement from a pastry brush to a food processor, I highly recommend the following.

www.williams-sonoma.com

www.lakeland.co.uk

www.fantes.com

Caja China

www.lacajachina.com

www.shoplatintouch.com

Spit Roasters

www.sunshinebbqs.com

www.ohiosignature.com

www.grillpro.com

www.spitjack.com

Meat

Support your local butcher or farmer and buy locally, if possible.

McReynolds Farm
www.mcreynoldsfarms.com

Will supply a great pig direct to your door in the USA

Number One Pig
www.numberonepig.co.uk

Will supply a great pig direct to your door in the UK

Websites

www.foodandwine.com

www.foodnetwork.com

www.amazingribs.com

Recommended reading

The Butcher's Apprentice
Aliza Green
(Quarry Books, 2012)

The Cook's Book: Step-by-Step Techniques & Recipes for Success
Every Time from the World's Top Chefs
Jill Norman editor-in-chief, 2006, including
Marcus Wareing, Shaun Hill, Ken Hom, and
Charlie Trotter

ABOUT THE AUTHOR

Tom Rea grew up on a farm on the south coast of England, shooting, fishing, and foraging—and eating pretty well as a result. He has worked as a chef and trained other chefs all over southern England and France, including at the multi-award winning gastropub The Coach and Horses, and at the even more prestigious Jolly Sportsman. He also teaches people how to cook and cater for their own private parties in style. *How to Roast a Pig* is his first book.

ACKNOWLEDGMENTS

This book is dedicated to my Mum Bobbette Rea, the woman who gave me the world and still won't stop giving, no matter how much I tell her to stop. Further thanks have to go to the wonderful Emily Dubberley for making this all happen and to my highly talented photographer, Natasha Bidgood. Finally, I want to thank my dad, Tom Rea, Sr., and apologize for the pig in the tub, occupying his house with a two-week photo shoot, and for making him eat pork for dinner for a month.

This book is in memory of my doggy pal, Dumpling, who got so fat during the making of this, but never saw the launch party. Her antics were legendary and she will be missed.

Index